P9-APK-841

Suicidal Behavior

WITHDRAWN

About the Author

Richard McKeon PhD, MPH received his doctorate in Clinical Psychology from the University of Arizona, and a Master's of Public Health in Health Administration from Columbia University. He has spent most of his career working in community mental health, including 11 years as director of a psychiatric emergency service and four years as Associate Administrator/Clinical Director of a hospital based community mental health center in Newton, New Jersey. He established the first evidenced based treatment program for chronically suicidal borderline patients in the state of New Jersey utilizing Marsha Linehan's Dialectical Behavior Therapy. In 2001, he was awarded an American Psychological Association Congressional Fellowship and worked for United States Senator Paul Wellstone, covering health and mental health policy issues. He spent five years on the Board of the American Association of Suicidology as Clinical Division Director and has also served on the Board of the Division of Clinical Psychology of the American Pychological Association. He is currently a public health advisor on suicide prevention for the Substance Abuse and Mental Health Services Administration where he coordinates suicide prevention activities. He also serves as Co-Chair of the Federal Working Group on Suicide Prevention.

Advances in Psychotherapy – Evidence-Based Practice

Danny Wedding; PhD, MPH, Prof., St. Louis, MO
(Series Editor)
Larry Beutler; PhD, Prof., Palo Alto, CA
Kenneth E. Freedland; PhD, Prof., St. Louis, MO
Linda C. Sobell; PhD, ABPP, Prof., Ft. Lauderdale, FL
David A. Wolfe; PhD, Prof., Toronto
(Associate Editors)

The basic objective of this series is to provide therapists with practical, evidence-based treatment guidance for the most common disorders seen in clinical practice – and to do so in a "reader-friendly" manner. Each book in the series is both a compact "how-to-do" reference on a particular disorder for use by professional clinicians in their daily work, as well as an ideal educational resource for students and for practice-oriented continuing education.

The most important feature of the books is that they are practical and "reader-friendly:" All are structured similarly and all provide a compact and easy-to-follow guide to all aspects that are relevant in real-life practice. Tables, boxed clinical "pearls", marginal notes, and summary boxes assist orientation, while checklists provide tools for use in daily practice.

Suicidal Behavior

Richard T. McKeon
Former Clinical Division Director, American Association of Suicidology

Library of Congress Cataloging in Publication

is available via the Library of Congress Marc Database under the
LC Control Number 2008939655

Library and Archives Canada Cataloguing in Publication

McKeon, Richard T
    Suicidal behavior / Richard McKeon.

(Advances in psychotherapy--evidence-based practice)
Includes bibliographical references.
ISBN 978-0-88937-327-3

    1. Suicidal behavior--Prevention. 2. Suicidal behavior--Treatment.
I. Title. II. Series.

RC569.M41 2008   616.85'8445   C2008-906676-6

PUBLISHING OFFICES
USA: Hogrefe & Huber Publishers, 875 Massachusetts Avenue, 7th Floor,
              Cambridge, MA 02139
              Phone (866) 823-4726, Fax (617) 354-6875; E-mail info@hhpub.com
EUROPE: Hogrefe & Huber Publishers, Rohnsweg 25, 37085 Göttingen, Germany
              Phone +49 551 49609-0, Fax +49 551 49609-88, E-mail hh@hhpub.com

SALES & DISTRIBUTION
USA: Hogrefe & Huber Publishers, Customer Services Department,
              30 Amberwood Parkway, Ashland, OH 44805
              Phone (800) 228-3749, Fax (419) 281-6883, E-mail custserv@hhpub.com
EUROPE: Hogrefe & Huber Publishers, Rohnsweg 25, 37085 Göttingen, Germany
              Phone +49 551 49609-0, Fax +49 551 49609-88, E-mail hh@hhpub.com

OTHER OFFICES
CANADA: Hogrefe & Huber Publishers, 1543 Bayview Avenue, Toronto, Ontario M4G 3B5
SWITZERLAND: Hogrefe & Huber Publishers, Länggass-Strasse 76, CH-3000 Bern 9

Hogrefe & Huber Publishers
Incorporated and registered in the State of Washington, USA, and in Göttingen, Lower Saxony,
Germany

Printed and bound in the USA
ISBN 978-0-88937-327-3

Acknowledgments

I would like to acknowledge all those who have made this book possible, including the publisher, Hogrefe and Huber, and especially Robert Dimbleby for his patience and support. I would also like to thank series editor Danny Wedding for supporting the inclusion of a book on suicidal behavior in the series *Advances in Psychotherapy: Evidence Based Practice*. His guidance during the development of this manuscript was invaluable.

It is of particular importance for me to express my gratitude to all those who have shared their stories, their pain, and their hopes with me over the years, including all those I have worked with in community mental health. All that I know I learned from them. To all the colleagues I have worked with to prevent suicide, whether we have worked together in emergency rooms, or on conference calls, in therapy groups or in symposiums, thank you for sustaining me in our shared vision of reducing the tragic loss of lives to suicide. I must also acknowledge all those I have met who have survived the loss of a loved one to suicide, but who have utilized their grief to insist we must do better, and in so doing have transformed a nation.

Finally, this book would not have been possible without the support of my family. I would like to thank my wife, Liz, for her advice, love, editing and encouragement, my sister, Kathy, for her assistance, my mother, Ruth, for her continued interest and support, and my daughters Britt and Shauna, who are my sources of hope for the future.

Disclaimer

Dedication

This book is dedicated to the memory of United States Senator Paul David Wellstone. Paul was a passionate champion for suicide prevention, and a transforming influence on all those who knew him.

Table of Contents

1

Description

Suicide is a tragic end to an individual's life, a devastating loss to families and friends, a diminishment of our communities, and a public health crisis for our nation. For clinicians, losing a patient to suicide is probably our worst fear. In 2005, over 32,000 Americans died by suicide (Centers for Disease Control, 2008a). Worldwide, an estimated one million people die by suicide each year, more than are lost to homicide or to war (World Health Organization, 2000). Self-inflicted injury is estimated to account for 1.4% of the total burden of disease worldwide (World Federation for Mental Health, 2006). Yet, despite the magnitude of these losses, or perhaps because of the depth of our distress and uncertainty when confronted with acts of deliberate self-destruction, we have tended as a society to look away and not grapple with the issue of suicidal behavior, despite the tragic toll it exacts.

Worldwide, about a million people per year die by suicide, more than are lost to homicide or war

Kay Redfield Jamison (1999) has eloquently stated that in dealing with suicide, "The gap between what we know, and what we do, is lethal." In *Night Falls Fast* (1999), her first-person account of her struggles with intense suicidal urges, she emphasizes the powerful link between mental illness and suicide, and the disturbing reality that the majority of those who die by suicide have never received mental health treatment. Despite the fact that we know how to treat successfully many of the conditions that are risk factors for suicide, such as depression, substance abuse, and bipolar illness, so many of those who die by suicide never receive such treatment for these disorders (Luoma, Martin, & Pearson, 2002).

While the gap between what we know and what we do is undoubtedly lethal, it is also tragically true that there is a huge gap between what we know and what we need to know to prevent suicide more effectively. This gap is also lethal. For, example, we do not have research that confirms that inpatient treatment is effective in preventing suicide, let alone under what circumstances hospitalization might be effective. We lack this knowledge even though reliance on inpatient hospitalization is a cornerstone of how virtually all mental health systems respond to suicidal individuals. In the past decade, the face of inpatient care in the U.S. has drastically changed, with lengths of stay being dramatically shortened for all patients (Pottick, McAlpine, & Andelman, 2000). This has amounted to a major, uncontrolled experiment in how we treat suicidal people, yet we know little about the impact such massive changes have had. In addition, despite the fact that involuntary hospitalization laws across the U.S. utilize the concept of imminent risk, the research on acute risk factors for suicide measures risk in months, not in hours or days (Simon, 2006). We also know distressingly little about how to successfully engage people at risk in treatment. The Utah Youth Suicide study showed that even though 44% of youth who died by suicide and had received psychiatric diagnoses had been prescribed psychotropic medication, upon autopsy none of the youth were found to have either therapeutic or sub-therapeutic medication levels (Moskos, Olson, Halbern, Keller, & Gray, 2005), We also know that continuity of care after acute episodes of care such as emergency department visits and inpatient hospitalization is poor despite substantial evidence that these are high risk times (Appleby et al., 1999).

Suicide is a public health crisis that has not received the attention it deserves

The President's New Freedom Commission Report on Mental Health, *Achieving the Promise, Transforming Mental Health Care in America* (2003), described suicide as "A public health crisis that has not received the attention it deserves." At least in part as a result of our failure to treat suicide as the public health crisis it is, the evidence base is not as strong for much of our work as it needs to be. The Institute of Medicine (IOM), in its 2002 report, *Reducing Suicide: A National Imperative,* reviewed the status of our scientific understanding of the causes and prevention of suicide, and pointed out both the extensive knowledge we have as well as how much we need to learn. "Despite the extensive knowledge that research has provided regarding (suicide) risk and protective factors, we are still far from being able to integrate these factors so as to understand how they work in concert to evoke suicidal behavior or to prevent it." (Goldsmith, Pellmar, Kleinman, & Bunney, 2002, p. 3).

The fragmentary nature of the evidence is also due to the systematic exclusion of suicidal patients from randomized controlled trials of psychotherapies and medications. Thus, approaches to preventing suicide that are sound conceptually, such as treating underlying risk factors such as depression or substance abuse, are often silent on the question of whether by treating these conditions successfully we are also preventing suicide. In addition, demonstrating the effectiveness of any intervention in preventing suicide is challenging because the size of the study required to demonstrate that lives have been saved is enormous. For this reason, the Institute of Medicine (2002) recommended the establishment of nationwide population laboratories so that sufficient participants can be included in research studies to be able to detect if lives are being saved (Goldsmith et al., 2002).

More recently, the field has advanced the state of knowledge by examining the full range of suicidal behavior as an outcome variable, rather than focusing exclusively on deaths by suicide. Because suicidal behavior is much more common than death by suicide, research demonstrating the effectiveness of interventions is much more feasible. Both treatment and prevention studies have demonstrated reductions in suicidal behavior (Allmon, Armstrong, Heard, Linehan, & Suarez, 1991; Aseltine & DeMartino, 2004; Brown et al., 2005; May, Serna, Hurt, & De Bruyn, 2005). While some would argue that those who die by suicide are a very different population from those who attempt suicide, and that therefore findings based on research on suicide attempters cannot be generalized to those who die by suicide, recent research that highlights both the subsequent mortality and morbidity associated with suicide attempts (Beautrais, 2004) supports the importance of research focused on this population.

Both treatment and prevention studies have demonstrated reductions in suicidal behavior

Advances in related fields, such as violence research, have taken place in part because of a willingness to look at violent behavior as a continuum, rather than focusing solely on homicide. As a result, findings with significant clinical implications, such as the ability to assess the risk of violent behavior on inpatient units at the time of hospital admission (McNiel, Gregory, Lam, Binder, & Sullivan, 2003), have occurred in violence research but not yet in suicide research. Such findings in the violence risk literature suggest that while evidence identifying imminent risk for suicidal behavior may now be lacking, it may be possible to obtain this evidence.

Additional research has demonstrated reductions in suicidal thinking or in suicidal intent (Bruce et al., 2004; Gould, Kalafat, Harris, Munfalh, & Kleinman, 2007). While reducing suicidal ideation or intent certainly does not assure a concomitant reduction in suicide attempts or in death by suicide, such cognitive phenomena are clearly very meaningful intermediate variables as they are very likely preconditions for suicide attempts or death by suicide.

The nation's failure to focus on suicide prevention has begun to change. In 2001, the U.S. Department of Health and Human Services, on behalf of a coalition of Federal agencies and private nonprofit organizations, issued the National Strategy for Suicide Prevention (NSSP). The U.S. thus joined nations around the world that have begun to implement and evaluate national strategies. The NSSP contains 11 goals and 68 objectives as part of a comprehensive public health strategy to reduce suicide and suicide attempts. Improved research is one of these critical objectives. The National Strategy also contained numerous objectives that challenge the mental heath field to improve its readiness and capacity to prevent suicides. Implementation of these objectives holds promise for improving the treatment and management of suicidal people. These objectives include the routine incorporation of training in suicide risk assessment and management into graduate training programs and into continuing education programs.

The National Strategy challenges the mental heath field to improve its readiness and capacity to prevent suicides

Bongar (2002) reviewed how frequently formal training in the study of suicide or the assessment or treatment of suicidal patients was offered in graduate school training in the mental health professions and found that the frequency of such training ranged from 29–41% in studies of psychology, social work, and marriage and family therapy training programs. It is clear that many mental health professionals receive little or no formal training in suicide prevention. Yet, most Americans probably assume that when they go to see a mental health professional they are seeing someone who has been trained to assess, manage, and treat suicide risk and behavior.

Many mental health professionals receive little or no formal training in suicide prevention

Other crucial national strategy objectives emphasize the importance of developing guidelines for assessing and managing risk in mental health systems, for improving continuity of care of suicidal patients following discharge from emergency departments and inpatient psychiatric units, and for more effectively involving and educating families of patients who are at risk of suicide.

While students in graduate training in the mental health professions may all too often receive little training in suicide risk assessment, treatment, or management, this does not mean that students are not treating patients at significant risk. In fact, one study found that one in nine graduate students in psychology had experienced a patient's suicide at some point during their training, 40% of them prior to their internship (Kleespies, Penk, & Forsyth, 1993). Findings such as these underscore the importance of training for graduate students in suicide prevention, not only to be a competent mental health professional, but

1 in 9 psychology graduates students experienced a patient's suicide during their training

also for trainees to be adequately prepared to treat those suicidal patients they will encounter during their training.

Treating suicidal patients requires numerous skills and competencies, including skills in assessment, treatment planning, managing crises, and knowledge of applicable laws and regulations. All these must occur within the context of clinicians having a clear understanding of their own feelings, attitudes, and judgments regarding suicidal behavior. We all react strongly to witnessing self-destruction. These reactions are based on our own past personal and professional experiences, including our own or our family or friends' experience of suicidal behavior. Understanding these reactions is essential to competently treating suicidal individuals.

I first experienced the loss of a patient to suicide when I was a psychology intern. I was providing outpatient psychotherapy to a patient that our entire treatment team believed to be at high, continuing risk for suicide. The reason for this perception of elevated risk was solidly grounded in what we now know about heightened suicide risk. He had a past history of suicide attempts, and these attempts were high in lethality, including one attempt during which he cut his own throat. A past history of suicide attempts, particularly attempts that are high in potential lethality, is the single, strongest predictor of ultimate death by suicide (Hawton, 2005). This was a man who had clearly demonstrated that he had the capacity for lethal self-destruction. Because of an increase in his level of depression, hopelessness, and suicidal ideation, he was hospitalized on an inpatient psychiatric unit. While he was hospitalized, I needed to return to my university to defend my doctoral dissertation. Upon my return to my internship, I learned that he had been discharged from the inpatient unit to a day hospital, but had taken a fatal overdose within 48 hours of his discharge. This powerful personal experience made me appreciate something I would later learn from the literature: The period immediately after an inpatient discharge, indeed after any episode of acute care for suicidality, contains significant, but frequently unrecognized risk for suicide.

In this book, I use the phrase "died by suicide" rather than the more common term, "committed suicide." I use this term out of respect to the countless family members who have lost a loved one to suicide. They have pointed out that we frequently use the word commit in contexts such as "commit a crime" or "commit a sin," and that suicide, though in the past treated as both a crime as well as a sin, is neither.

1.1   Terminology

Suicidal thoughts and behavior are not limited to any single diagnostic group or condition

Suicidal thoughts or behavior are not limited to any single diagnostic group or condition. Death by suicide occurs with distressing frequency among many different illnesses, including mood disorders, substance abuse disorders, schizophrenia, and personality disorders. The Institute of Medicine (2002) summarized the state of research in suicide and suicide prevention and reported that in the U.S. over 90% of suicides are associated with mental illness or substance abuse disorders (Goldsmith et al, 2002).

Table 1
DSM-IV TR diagnoses that include suicidal behavior

Diagnostic criteria for 296.xx Major Depressive Episode:

Criteria 9 – recurrent thoughts of suicide (not just fear of dying), recurrent suicidal ideation without specific plan, or a suicide attempt or a specific plan for committing suicide

Diagnostic criteria for 301.83 Borderline Personality Disorder

Criteria 5 – recurrent suicidal behavior, gestures, threats, or self-mutilating behavior

Suicidal behavior is not a DSM-IV TR diagnoses, although two DSM-IV TR diagnoses reference suicidality (see Table 1). The International Classification of Diseases, 9th Revision, Clinical Modification (ICD-9-CM) includes codes for classifying external causes of injury (E-codes). These codes are an important mechanism for surveillance of suicide attempts, particularly in hospital settings, and are used to distinguish between intentional and nonintentional injuries. The ICD also provides codes for overdose and poisoning in an appendix labeled "overdose." These are used to code this frequent method for suicide attempts, as well as to code for accidental overdoses.

1.2 Definition

As suicidal behaviors are not DSM-IV TR diagnoses, the diagnostic manual has not been the definitive source for definition and nomenclature that it has been in other areas of mental health. This has been the source of significant confusion. While many nations do have surveillance systems to monitor deaths by suicide, no national or international surveillance system exists for monitoring suicide attempts and estimating national rates of occurrence (Silverman, Berman, Sanddal, O'Carroll, & Joiner, 2007a) despite the significance of suicidal behavior as both a clinical and public health issue. In addition, many confusing terms and inconsistencies exist in both the research and clinical literatures (Silverman et al., 2007a)

A pivotal event in the development of terminology occurred in 1970, when the Center for the Study of Suicide Prevention of the National Institute of Mental Health convened a committee on classification chaired by Aaron Beck (Brown, Jeglic, Henriques, & Beck, 2006). A classification system was developed that included the categories of completed suicide, suicide attempts, and suicidal ideation. Suicidal intent was identified as a critical variable in this classification scheme. For a self-injurious behavior to be considered a suicide attempt, suicidal intent was necessary (Beck et al., 1973). Self-injurious behavior was the recommended term when there was no suicidal intent associated with the behavior (Beck et al., 1973).

One challenge for this system has been that suicidal intent, which is essential for determining whether a death by suicide or suicide attempt has occurred, can be very difficult to determine. Self-report on intent after an attempt can be

Self-report of suicidal intent can be unreliable and heavily influenced by the perceived consequences of acknowledging intent to die

Suicidal intent can fluctuate over time and be fraught with ambivalence

unreliable and heavily influenced by context and the potential consequences for patients of acknowledging suicidal intent. In addition, suicidal intent can also fluctuate over time and be fraught with ambivalence. Despite these challenges, the nomenclature has met many clinical needs, and terms like suicidal ideation and suicidal intent have become familiar to virtually all clinicians. However, this terminology has proved inadequate for research purposes, leading nomenclature in this field to be described as a "Tower of Babel" (Silverman et al., 2007a) as studies have used varying definitions of terms such as suicide attempt. Such variability in definition has made comparability across studies extremely difficult.

Recently, a revised nomenclature has been proposed (Silverman, Berman, Sanddal, O'Carroll, & Joiner, 2007b). While a key goal of this revision was to help advance research, the revision was also "designed to serve as an instrument to assist clinicians in better identifying those most at risk for suicide related behaviors in order to keep them alive" (Silverman et al., 2007b, p.274). The revision affirms the crucial role of suicidal intent, and, recognizing the inherently difficult nature of determining intent, utilizes three categories of no intent, uncertain intent, and intent. This replaces the prior dichotomy of suicide attempts versus self-injury. A suicide attempt is defined as a self-inflicted, potentially injurious behavior with a nonfatal outcome for which there is evidence of intent to die (Silverman et al., 2007b). The term "undetermined suicide-related behavior" is used when suicide intent is uncertain. Self-harm is used rather than self-injury when it is clear there is no suicidal intent. This classification system thus explicitly deals with those problematic situations where intent is difficult or impossible to determine.

A suicide plan is a systematic formulation of a program of action that has the potential to lead to self-injury

Suicide plan is another term frequently used in clinical practice but often not defined clearly. In fact, there is a tendency to equate having a suicide plan with having a suicide method. While thinking about what method to use in a suicide attempt is clearly subsumed under the notion of planning, by equating them, much important assessment information is often missed. There may be other significant preparatory behaviors taking place (e.g., writing a suicide note, giving away possessions), and simply knowing whether a person has thought of a method tells us nothing about the degree of planning, forethought, and mental rehearsal the person has devoted to the possibility of killing himself or herself. In this proposed nomenclature, a suicide plan is described more broadly as "a systematic formulation of a program of action that has the potential to lead to self-injury" (Silverman et al., 2007b).

Another common term in clinical usage is *suicide gesture*. Suicide gesture typically refers to a circumstance in which overt suicidal behavior takes place

Clinical Vignette
Systematic Planning for Suicide

John told several high school friends he was planning on killing himself that night. Alarmed, one of his friends told a parent, who in turn contacted the mental health center. When evaluated, it was discovered that John had obtained a large stash of pills with which to overdose, had given away some of his prized records and other possessions, and had picked out the clothes he wanted to be found in when his body was discovered. He exhibited detailed, systematic planning for his suicide. He was assessed as being at high, imminent risk and was hospitalized.

but the person's intent is judged by others to be an attempt to communicate distress rather than reflecting true intent to die. These "gestures" are frequently labeled as manipulative. Such terms are pejorative and can lead clinician's to assume the absence of potential lethality prior to a thorough assessment being completed. The proposed nomenclature recommends against the use of the term suicide gesture because of this pejorative implication (Silverman et al, 2007b). The term should be avoided.

The proposed Silverman et al. (2007b) nomenclature is shown in Table 2. In addition to the important role of suicidal intent, the nomenclature also incorporates whether or not the outcome of a suicidal act is a fatal or nonfatal injury. There can be very serious suicide attempts that do not lead to injury. For example, a person who points a loaded gun at themselves and deliberately pulls the trigger has clearly made a suicide attempt, even if the gun jams and there is no resulting injury.

The term "suicide gesture" can lead clinician's to assume the absence of potential lethality prior to conducting a thorough assessment

Table 2
Nomenclature For Suicide Related-Behavior

Nomenclature for Suicide-Related Behavior			Intent to Die by Suicide	Outcomes		
				No Injury	Non-Fatal Injury	Death
Suicide-Related Behavior	Self-Harm	With No Suicidal Intent				
		Without Injuries Self-Harm – Type I	No	√		
		With Injuries Self-Harm – Type II	No		√	
		With Fatal Injuries Self-Inflicted Unintentional Death	No			√
	Undetermined Suicide-Related Behavior	With Undetermined Suicidal Intent				
		Without Injuries Undetermined Suicide-Related Behavior – Type I	Undetermined	√		
		With Injuries Undetermined Suicide-Related Behavior – Type II	Undetermined		√	
		With Fatal Injuries Self-Inflicted Death with Undetermined Intent	Undetermined			√
	Suicide Attempt	With Suicidal Intent				
		Without Injuries Suicide Attempt – Type I	Yes	√		
		With Injuries Suicide Attempt – Type II	Yes		√	
		With Fatal Injuries Suicide	Yes			√

An additional classification system for suicidal events has been proposed by Posner, Oquendo, Gould, Stanley, and Davies (2007). In response to the recent controversy that has swirled around possible links between the use of selective serotonin reuptake inhibitors (SSRIs) and suicidality, the Food and Drug Administration (FDA) commissioned Columbia University to review adverse events involving suicidality in the randomized controlled trials performed by the pharmaceutical companies in the development of the medications. In order to accomplish this, the Columbia Classification Algorithm of Suicide Assessment (C-CASA) was developed, along with the Columbia Suicide Severity Rating Scale (CSSRS). In this system as well, suicidal intent plays a critical role. This system also utilizes terms with clinical utility, such as preparatory action toward imminent suicidal behavior, which can include actions such as purchasing pills to overdose or writing a suicide note. This system also utilizes the terms aborted and interrupted suicide attempts. An aborted suicide attempt is when an attempt is stopped by the person themselves, for example, taking out pills or a firearm to use in an attempt and then deciding not to go through with it. An interrupted attempt is when the attempt is stopped by some other person. In this system, there are essentially four categories rather than the traditional three categories of suicidal ideation, attempts, and deaths by suicide; the fourth category being preparatory behaviors, where the line between ideation and action has been crossed, but short of an action that could cause injury. This system also distinguishes between wish to die without suicidal ideation, specific ideation versus general ideation, and planning versus method.

> **Preparatory action toward imminent suicidal behavior crosses the line between ideation and action**

With the support of the Centers for Disease Control, a working group is currently attempting to reach a consensus on these important definitional issues,

1.3   Differential Diagnosis

The differential diagnosis of suicide attempts versus self-harm or self-injury can be complex for a number of reasons (see Table 3). First, there may be no overt behavioral differences to distinguish between them. Rather, the critical difference involves the presence or absence of suicidal intent. If the person tells us that he intended to die when he cut his wrists, we will call it a suicide attempt. If he tells us he did not wish to die, but rather that he was attempting to distract himself from emotional pain, or to punish himself, we will call it self-harm, self-mutilation, or self injury. In either instance we are relying mostly on the individual's self-report regarding his intent. However, some people who have suicidal intent may deny it because of concern they will be hospitalized or because of shame or embarrassment. Others may claim suicidal intent when in reality there was none, feeling that otherwise what they have done may be minimized or invalidated by others. And this distinction presumes that a person was clear at the time of his or her self-destructive act regarding his or her intentions. It also presumes he or she is remembering it clearly, since such acts frequently take place during moments of intense emotional dysregulation (Linehan, 1993).

Table 3
Differential Diagnosis of Suicide Attempts Versus Self-Harm

SELF-HARM (with no suicidal intent) Similar terms: self-mutilation, deliberate self-harm, self injury		
	Similarities	**Differences**
Self-harm with no suicidal intent	Intentional act (may result in fatal or nonfatal injuries)	No intent to die (may be a variety of different intents, such as reduce pain, punish self)
Suicide attempt	Intentional act (may result in fatal or nonfatal injuries)	Intent to die

The following are examples of self-harm with no suicidal intent, a suicide attempt with clear suicidal intent, and a suicide-related behavior with undetermined intent.

Clinical Vignettes
Role of Suicidal Intent

Self Harm with No Suicidal Intent

A physical education teacher noticed during gym class that Julie was trying to conceal multiple cuts on her arms. When interviewed later by the school psychologist, she admitted to cutting herself repeatedly to "relieve my pain." She denied any thoughts about wanting to die or kill herself.

Suicide Attempt with Clear Suicidal Intent

Richard had a long history of depression and alcohol abuse. Following his third arrest for driving while intoxicated, which would trigger the loss of his driver's license, which in turn would force him to quit his job, he took an overdose of approximately 40 of his anti-depressants and went to bed, fully expecting he would die in his sleep. In the middle of the night his wife found him stumbling around the bedroom delirious and called 911. When interviewed in the emergency department he reported being upset he was still alive.

Suicide-Related Behavior with Undetermined Intent

Harold was a 31-year-old Caucasian male. Since the onset of legal problems that had been pending over a period of many months, he had been experiencing recurrent suicidal ideation. Intensive outpatient therapy had averted a hospitalization, but he was still being monitored carefully for suicidal risk. While on vacation, he experienced what was presumed to be a serious skiing accident. After a number of days in the hospital for his injuries, he returned to psychotherapy. Since Harold was an excellent skier, his therapist talked with him about how this had happened. Harold acknowledged that he had been having thoughts about suicide that day, but that he had made no plan to kill himself. He reported that as he was skiing down the hill he went around a curve and left the trail and crashed into a tree at high speed. He did not recall making a conscious decision to try to die. He also didn't know if his wish to die had led him to be less careful and less focused on his safety. He was genuinely uncertain about his suicidal intent

Presuming the meaning/intent of a self-destructive act based on past history can bias assessment

Another complication in making a differential assessment is that the same person may engage in both suicide attempts and self-harm with no suicidal intent. Therefore each person needs to be assessed without presuming that because they have a history of "self-mutilation" suicidal intent is not present at the current time. Presuming to know the meaning or intent of a self-destructive act based on past history and allowing this to bias the assessment is a clinical error. Another error in clinical reasoning is to make a judgment about intent based on the degree of lethality of the actions taken. Persons who take an overdose of a few pills or who make superficial cuts should not be presumed to be without suicidal intent based on the lack of lethality of their actions. The person may have misjudged the lethality of her behavior, or may have very serious suicidal intent and be working up the resolve to make a more lethal attempt.

Persons who make low lethality attempts should not be presumed to be without suicidal intent

While suicidality and self-harm may seem inextricably interwoven, there are different implications for these two behaviors. Suicide attempts are more likely to lead to psychiatric hospitalization than self-harm without suicidal intent. Self-mutilation is more likely to occur with greater frequency, at times in an almost addictive spiral, compared to suicide attempts. Such distinctions, as well as others, have led Walsh (2006) to argue that the two conditions should be understood, managed, and treated differently. When a person only has a history of self-harm, it is tempting to assume that each repeated episode of harm is unlikely to be a suicide attempt. However, it is hazardous, even for an individual with a history of solely self-harm without suicidal intent, to assume that all future episodes are without suicidal ideation or intent. In a study in England in which patients seen in emergency departments for episodes of deliberate self-harm were followed up over time, the suicide rate was 36 times that for the general population (Cooper et al., 2005). There was no difference in the suicide rate between those who had reported suicidal intent and those who had not, highlighting the hazard of assuming that those who engage in self-harm without suicidal intent are not at risk, at least for those whose self-harm is serious enough to warrant emergency care. The clinician must always assess, not assume. Such cases must be managed and assessed considering the potential for suicide risk, at least until the assessment has made clear that there is low risk.

Clinicians must always assess, not assume

Clinical Vignette
Assessing Suicidal Intent

Eileen was a 55-year-old, married, Irish-American female with a diagnosis of borderline personality disorder and recurrent major depressions. She was referred to the clinic for dialectical behavior therapy. She had a history of many episodes of self-harm without suicidal intent, as well as several suicide attempts, some utilizing potentially lethal methods such as hanging. During the course of treatment she made additional suicide attempts as well as episodes of self-harm without suicidal intent, although the frequency of such episodes declined over time with continuing treatment. Assessment around these episodes revealed that there were times that there was clear suicidal intent, there were times that suicidal intent was clearly absent, and there were times that in the throes of emotional dysregulation, Eileen was simply unsure what her intent had been.

1.4   Epidemiology

The epidemiology of suicidal behavior, particularly deaths by suicide, has been studied extensively, both in the U.S. as well as in many countries around the world. In the year 2000, there were over 100,000 deaths by suicide in India, and more than 170,000 in China (WHO, 2000). However, to fully understand the impact that suicidality represents to our society, it is important to understand the different levels of suicidal behavior that exist, including deaths by suicide, suicide attempts, and suicidal thinking, and the burden these impose, including the costs of hospitalizations and emergency department visits.

Over 30,000 Americans die by suicide each year. Significantly more Americans die by suicide than by homicide, by a 3 to 2 ratio.

Significantly more Americans die by suicide than by homicide

According to the most recent data available from the Centers for Disease Control (CDC, 2008a), suicide is the eleventh leading cause of death for all ages, accounting for 1.3% of all deaths in the U.S. Suicide is the eighth leading cause of death among males, and the seventeenth leading cause of death among females. For some age groups, suicide ranks even higher as a leading cause of death. Suicide is the second leading cause of death among 25–34-year-olds and the third leading cause of death among 15–24-year olds (CDC, 2008a). Among 15–24-year olds, suicide accounts for 12.3% of all deaths (CDC, 2008a).

More than 32,000 suicides occurred in the U.S. in 2005, a rate of 11.05 suicides per 100,000 population (CDC, 2008a). This is the equivalent of 89 suicides per day; or one suicide every **16** minutes.

An American dies by suicide every 16 minutes

Males outnumber females in suicide deaths by a ratio of almost four to one. Among males, adults aged 75 years and older have the highest rate of suicide – 37.97 per 100,000 (CDC, 2008à). Among females, those in their 40s and 50s have the highest rate of suicide – 7.53 per 100,000 (CDC, 2008a). In the past, suicide rates, particularly for males, increased in a linear fashion with age, this effect has been moderated in recent years.

Suicide Deaths
32,637

Hospitalizations
115,860

Emergency Department Visits
420,000

CDC, 2008

Figure 1
Self-directed violence – United States, 2005

Firearms are the most commonly used method of suicide among males

Poisoning is the most common method of suicide for females

Firearms are the most commonly used method of suicide among males – 57.6% (CDC, 2008a), while poisoning is the most common method of suicide for females – 39.1% (CDC, 2008a). An increase in the number of suicides using hanging has also been reported by the CDC, particularly among youth (CDC, 2007).

In the US, suicide risk is highest among Caucasians, American Indians, and Alaska Natives. American Indian and Alaska Native youth and young adults have particularly high suicide rates.

For both fatal and nonfatal self-harm, injury rates begin to rise sharply at ages 13 and 14 (Vajani, Annest, Crosby, Alexander, & Millet, 2007).

While the highest rates of suicide are found among the elderly, particularly those over the age of 75, the greatest number of suicides in the U.S. takes place in midlife, particularly among males. This is because this cohort (which includes the "baby boom" generation) is more populous. This points out the hazards of adapting epidemiologic data to clinical practice without careful analysis. Assigning risk to groups in the population tends to be interpreted in relation to the U.S. average, but it is critical to remember that even if a group has a lower suicide rate than the national average this does not mean that hundreds, if not thousands, from that demographic group may not die by suicide every year. For example, the fact that significantly more males than females die by suicide does not mean that clinicians should not be alert to suicide risk in women. In fact, more than 50% of female suicides occur among those receiving mental health treatment (CDC, 2008b), underscoring the importance for clinicians of being alert to the potential for suicide in women. Suicide among those in midlife is a concern, not only because of the large numbers of deaths by suicide in this age group, but also because of recent increases in the suicide rate (American Association of Suicidology, 2008).

More than 50% of U.S. women who died by suicide were being treated for a mental health problem

The epidemiology of suicide attempts differs in important respects from deaths by suicide. Unfortunately, surveillance data on suicide attempts has been less available than data on death by suicide. In the US, there is no official national estimate of the number of suicide attempts. The various estimates that do exist of the numbers of suicide attempts nationally vary widely depending on the source of data. A common estimate is that there is a 25 to one ratio between nonfatal suicide attempts and deaths by suicide. If this estimate is correct then the number of suicide attempts in the US is approximately 800,000 annually (American Association of Suicidology, 2008). The most conservative measures are based on cases seen and counted in the healthcare system. In 2005, 420,000 people were treated in emergency departments (EDs) for self-inflicted injuries and 115,860 people were hospitalized due to self-inflicted injury (McCaig & Nawar, 2006). These figures represent neither the total numbers of persons hospitalized or seen in EDs because of suicidality, as those seen in these acute settings because of suicidal ideation are not included, nor does it represent the total number of attempted suicides, as not all suicide attempts receive medical attention

The ratio of deaths by suicide to suicide attempts varies dramatically with age. Among young adults ages 15 to 24 years old, there is 1 suicide for every 100–200 attempts (Goldsmith et al., 2002). Among adults ages 65 years and older, there is 1 suicide for every 4 suicide attempts (Goldsmith et al., 2002).

Table 4
10 Leading Causes of Death by Age Group, United States – 2003

Rank	<1	1–4	5–9	10–14	15–24	25–34	35–44	45–54	55–65	65+	Total
						Age Groups					
1	Congenital Anomalies 5,621	Unintentional Injury 1,717	Unintentional Injury 1,096	Unintentional Injury 1,522	Unintentional Injury 15,272	Unintentional Injury 12,541	Unintentional Injury 16,766	Malignant Neoplasms 49,843	Malignant Neoplasms 95,692	Heart Disease 563,390	Heart Disease 685,089
2	Short Gestation 4,849	Congenital Anomalies 541	Malignant Neoplasms 516	Malignant Neoplasms 560	Homicide 5,368	Suicide 5,065	Malignant Neoplasms 15,509	Heart Disease 37,732	Heart Disease 65,060	Malignant Neoplasms 388,911	Malignant Neoplasms 556,902
3	SIDS 2,162	Malignant Neoplasms 392	Congenital Anomalies 180	Suicide 244	Suicide 3,988	Homicide 4,516	Heart Disease 13,600	Unintentional Injury 15,837	Chronic Low. Respiratory Disease 12,077	Cerebrovascular 136,134	Cerebrovascular 157,689
4	Maternal Pregnancy Comp. 1,710	Homicide 376	Homicide 122	Congenital Anomalies 206	Malignant Neoplasms 1,651	Malignant Neoplasms 3,741	Suicide 6,602	Liver Disease 7,466	Diabetes Mellitus 10,731	Chronic Low. Respiratory Disease 109,139	Chronic Low. Respiratory Disease 126,382
5	Placenta Cord Membranes 1,069	Heart Disease 186	Heart Disease 104	Heart Disease 160	Heart Disease 1,133	Heart Disease 3,250	HIV 5,340	Suicide 6,481	Cerebrovascular 9,946	Alzheimer's Disease 62,814	Unintentional Injury 109,277
6	Unintentional Injury 945	Influenza & Pneumonia 163	Influenza & Pneumonia 75	Chronic Low. Respiratory Disease 81	Congenital Anomalies 451	HIV 1,588	Homicide 3,110	Cerebrovascular 6,127	Unintentional Injury 9,170	Influenza & Pneumonia 57,670	Diabetes Mellitus 74,219
7	Respiratory Distress 831	Septicemia 85	Septicemia 39	Influenza & Pneumonia 72	Influenza & Pneumonia 224	Diabetes Mellitus 657	Liver Disease 3,020	Diabetes Mellitus 5,658	Liver Disease 6,428	Diabetes Mellitus 54,919	Influenza & Pneumonia 65,163
8	Bacterial Sepsis 772	Perinatal Period 79	Benign Neoplasms 38	Benign Neoplasms 41	Cerebrovascular 221	Cerebrovascular 583	Cerebrovascular 2,460	HIV 4,442	Suicide 3,843	Nephritis 35,254	Alzheimer's Disease 63,457
9	Neonatal Hemorrhage 649	Chronic Low. Respiratory Disease 55	Chronic Low. Respiratory Disease 37	Benign Neoplasms 41	Chronic Low. Respiratory Disease 191	Congenital Anomalies 426	Diabetes Mellitus 2,049	Chronic Low. Respiratory Disease 3,537	Nephritis 3,806	Unintentional Injury 34,335	Nephritis 42,453
10	Circulatory System Disease 591	Benign Neoplasms 51	Cerebrovascular 29	Cerebrovascular 40	HIV 178	Influenza & Pneumonia 373	Influenza & Pneumonia 992	Viral Hepatitis 2,259	Septicemia 3,651	Septicemia 26,445	Septicemia 34,069

Source: National Vital Statistics System, National Center for Health Statistics, CDC. Produced by: Office of Statistics and Programming, National Center for Injury Prevention and Control, CDC.

Table 5
YRBS Suicidal Thoughts And Behavior: Students 9–12th Grade (2007)

Seriously Considered Suicide in the previous 12 months	Made at least one suicide attempt in the past 12 months	Made at least one suicide attempt in the past 12 months that required medical attention
14.5%	6.9%	2.0%

Other estimates of suicide attempts come from the Youth Risk Behavior Survey (YRBS), a U.S., school based survey utilizing a self report instrument conducted by the Centers for Disease Control, and from the National Survey of Drug Use and Health (NSDUH), a household interview, conducted by the Substance Abuse and Mental Health Services Administration (SAMHSA).

The YRBS monitors risk behaviors that contribute to the leading causes of death, disability, and social problems among youth in the U.S. The YRBS is conducted every two years and provides data representative of 9th through 12th grade students in public and private schools throughout the U.S.

In 2007 (see Table 5; CDC, 2008c)), 14.5% of students, grades 9–12, had seriously considered suicide in the previous 12 months (18.7% of females and 10.3% of males; CDC, 2008c). In that year, 6.9% of students reported making at least one suicide attempt (9.3% of females and 4.6% of males), while 2.0% of students reported making at least one suicide attempt in the previous 12 months that required medical attention (2.4% of females and 1.5% of males; CDC, 2008c). Based on these findings, it appears that a significant majority of those who attempt suicide, at least among youth, never come to the attention of the health care system.

14.5% of high school students report they have seriously considered suicide within the past 12 months

The SAMHSA National Survey on Drug Use and Health reported that an estimated 14% of youths aged 12 to 17, approximately 3.5 million young people, had experienced at least one major depressive episode in their lifetime (SAMHSA, 2006a). Over 7%, an estimated 1.8 million youths, had thought about killing themselves at the time of their worst or most recent episode. An estimated 712,000 youths had tried to kill themselves during their worst or most recent major depressive episode; this represents 2.9% of those aged 12 to 17, a figure similar to that reported in the YRBS.

Data on suicide attempts and related behaviors are also available on adults from the NSDUH . Among adults who experienced a major depressive episode in the past year, 56.3% thought during their worst or most recent episode that it would be better if they were dead, 40.3% thought about suicide, 14.5% made a suicide plan, and 10.4% made a suicide attempt (SAMHSA, 2006b).

Recent major advances in knowledge have resulted from the implementation in 17 states of the National Violent Death Reporting System (NVDRS). Operated in coordination with the Centers for Disease Control, the NVDRS is able to provide state wide data on characteristics of people who die by suicide that were previously not available because most data on deaths by suicide were derived from death certificates. Death certificates only contain basic information such as age, sex, race, and cause of death. Hence we have not had systematic epidemiological data on questions such as the prevalence of suicide among military veterans, the frequency of homicide/suicides, or how often those who have died by suicide have received prior mental health treatment. By linking death certificate data with data from police reports and laboratory findings, our knowledge is being substantially enhanced. For example, we now estimate that approximately 20% of those who die by suicide are either current or former U.S. military personnel and know that combined homicide/suicides occur most frequently in the context of domestic violence.

1.5   Course and Prognosis

Suicide is not a disorder per se with a clear course and prognosis. The "course" varies depending on whether one is analyzing populations having suicidal thoughts, those making suicide attempts, or those who have died by suicide. The pattern differs still if one is examining those disorders that are associated with increased suicide risk, such as affective disorders, substance abuse, or personality disorders. Yet some conclusions can be drawn. First, suicide is never inevitable. No matter how high the risk for an individual, no matter how deep and realistic the clinician's level of concern, there is always hope. The absence of hope on the part of a clinician that a patient can survive his or her suicidal impulses is a powerful signal of the need for consultation.

A clinician who feels hopeless that a patient can survive his or her suicidal impulses needs to obtain a consultation

The epidemiology is clear: Many more people think about suicide than act on those thoughts. And, of those who act on those thoughts, many more make nonfatal suicide attempts than die by suicide. While all those who make either fatal or nonfatal suicide attempts must have previously thought about it, not all those who die by suicide have made a previous attempt. Perhaps 30–40% of those who die by suicide progress from thought to nonfatal suicidal behavior to fatal suicidal behavior (Maris, 1992). But for others who make suicide attempts, some will never again engage in suicidal behavior, while others will make subsequent, multiple additional attempts but not die by suicide. Maris (1981) estimated that approximately 15% of suicide attempters go on to die by suicide. The critical trajectory is thus from suicidal thoughts to suicidal behavior.

30–40% of suicide deaths are preceded by a suicide attempt

15% of those who attempt suicide will go on to die by suicide

Suicidal ideation is relatively common. The YRBS (2008c) shows that almost 15% of youths reported seriously considering suicide within the last year. The NSDUH (2006) showed that 40% of adults with major depressive episodes wanted to kill themselves during their worst or most recent episode, and 10% made suicide attempts. Thus, thoughts about killing oneself are almost normative for those suffering from major depression; however, only a minority will take the next step and engage in suicidal behavior.

Thoughts about killing oneself are almost normative for those suffering from major depression

When one examines the topography of suicidal thoughts and scrutinizes the full continuum of these phenomena, from a passive longing for death to suicidal intent and plans, a clear intensification can be seen. As Shneidman (1996) describes it, "The mind scans its options: the topic of suicide comes up, the mind rejects it, scans again, there is suicide, it is rejected again, and then finally the mind accepts suicide as a solution, then plans it, then fixes on it as the only answer" (p. 15). The same person at the end of this process is clearly more at risk than at the start. Though both can be described as having "suicidal ideation," the person at the end of this process has suicidal ideation, suicidal intent, and a suicide plan. Jamison (1999) puts this same process in more evocative language, "If it has ever been taken up as an option, the black knight has a tendency to remain in play" (p. 4).

While it is clear that suicidal thoughts can intensify in terms of frequency and duration, and that planning for suicide can become more elaborate and more specific, there is little research to describe how these processes develop into lethal actions. There is also limited research helping us understand how a person develops suicidal intent, where there is not only thinking about suicide, but also "a resolve to act" (Silverman et al., 2007a).

There is evidence that the prevalence of suicide planning more closely resembles suicide attempts than suicidal ideation. Among those with major depressive episodes, 56.3% thought during their worst or most recent episode that they would be better off dead, 40.3% thought about dying by suicide, while 14.5% made a suicide plan, and 10.4% made an attempt (SAMHSA, 2006).

60% of transitions from ideation to first attempt were within the first year after the onset of suicidal ideation

The next step, once the "black knight" is in play, is moving from thought to action, from considering self-destruction to attempting it. In a cross-national study, 60% of the transitions from suicidal ideation to first suicide attempt occurred within the first year since the onset of suicidal ideation (Nock et al., 2008). In a study of suicidal ideators who went on to make suicide attempts over a 12 month period, those who had made a suicide plan were significantly more likely to make a suicide attempt than those who had not made a plan (Borges et al., 2006).

Since, on average, over their lifetimes, approximately 10–15% of those who make a nonfatal suicide attempt eventually go on to kill themselves (Maris, 1992), a suicide attempt is certainly not an inevitable harbinger of death by suicide. However, since 30–40% of those who ultimately die by suicide have made a previous attempt, this makes a prior suicide attempt the single strongest risk factor for death by suicide (Hawton, 2005). However, there is significant variation by age and gender. For example, Maris (1992) reports that 88% of males over the age of 45 made only a single, fatal attempt, while among youth suicide attempts greatly outnumber deaths by suicide.

A prior suicide attempt is the single strongest risk factor for death by suicide

In addition, those who make suicide attempts vary in the number of suicide attempts made. In a survey by Maris (1992), of those who died by suicide and had made a prior suicide attempt, 70% had made one prior attempt, approximately 14% had made two previous attempts, and the rest had made three attempts or more.

Recent research has further demonstrated the significant mortality and morbidity associated with suicide attempts. In a five-year follow-up, Beautrais (2004) found that of 302 individuals who made a medically serious suicide attempt, almost half (44.5%) either made another suicide attempt or died by suicide. The mortality rate from suicide over that 5-year period was 6.7%, while more than 37% made an additional nonfatal suicide attempt. Those who made additional suicide attempts were more likely to have made a suicide attempt in the five years prior to the index attempt and to have had a psychiatric admission in the previous year (Beautrais, 2004). Of particular significance,

Beautrais also found that among those who died by suicide, a significant number (75%) changed from the method used at the index attempt to a more lethal method that resulted in their death. This is strong evidence that many who die by suicide escalate the lethality of their actions over time, a point emphasized in recent work by Thomas Joiner (2005), who argues that people who die by suicide must acquire the capacity to inflict lethal self-harm by becoming gradually desensitized to this fearsome behavior.

Many who died by suicide utilized increasingly lethal methods in comparison to the index attempt

Beautrais argues that suicide attempters should receive intensive follow-up services, particularly in light of the difficulty in identifying characteristics of attempters that would predict later death. The only such characteristic able to be identified was, in the immediate aftermath of the attempt, the person attempting suicide regretted survival and still wanted to die.

Regretting surviving a serious suicide attempt should be considered a very important sign of future risk

In a prospective cohort study of 7,968 ER patients seen for deliberate self-harm, the suicide rate in the following year was 371 per 100,000, approximately 34 times the expected rate (Cooper et al., 2005). Suicide rates were highest within the next six months following the index self-harm episode. Independent predictors of subsequent suicide were engaging in efforts to avoid discovery at the time of the episode, alcohol misuse, and not living with close relatives. Whether the self-injury was intended as a suicide attempt was not a significant predictor of subsequent suicide in this study.

While some will make a suicide attempt and never attempt again, others will make further attempts, escalating in lethality, until ultimate death by suicide. It is of critical importance that multiple suicide attempters be viewed as a very high risk population in need of intensive treatment. In the study of Beautrais (2004), over a quarter (26.2%) made four or more attempts within a five-year period. These findings rebut the stereotype that multiple suicide attempters are not "seriously" suicidal and engage only in low lethality suicidal behavior. At the same time, the absence of this kind of history of suicidal behavior cannot be viewed as assurance that someone is not at risk for suicide. Particularly among older persons, the first suicide attempt may be fatal.

When examining those who have attempted suicide without regard to the lethality of the attempt, Owens, Horrocks and House (2002) found that 23% had made further attempts and 3.4% had died by suicide upon four-year follow-up. Gibb, Beautrais, and Ferguson (2005), when looking at hospitalized suicide attempters regardless of lethality level, found 28.1% were re-admitted for a further suicide attempt, and 4.6% died by suicide, leading these researchers to the conclusion that the risk of subsequent suicide and further suicide attempts following an index suicide attempt is higher for all those who attempt suicide, regardless of the medical severity of the attempt.

An important contribution to the literature on the circumstances preceding lethal and near lethal suicidal behavior was the Houston Case Control Study of Nearly Lethal Suicide Attempts (Simon, Swann, Powell, Potter, Kresnow, & O'Carroll, 2001) This study found that up to 24% of nearly lethal suicide attempters had spent less than 5 minutes between the decision to attempt suicide and the actual nearly lethal suicide attempt. In fact, 5% reported spending only one second (Simon et al., 2001). The association of these near-lethal impulsive suicide attempts with physical fighting, particularly among males, suggests a potential role of intense emotional dysregulation. While on the surface the

Up to 24% of nearly lethal suicide attempters spent less than 5 minutes between the decision and the act itself

findings of Simon et al. (2001) may make it seem that many suicide attempts "come out of the blue" and are spontaneous, impulsive acts, it is quite possible that such impulsive acts were actually preceded by a period of thinking and planning that ultimately reached an apparently sudden "tipping point" (Goldney, 1998). The fact that approximately one-third of these impulsive, near lethal attempters reported telling someone that they were considering suicide (Simon et al., 2001) supports this notion. For the entire sample of persons making near lethal suicide attempts, 48% had sought help from family or friends (Barnes, Ikeda, & Kresnow, 2001) in the month prior to the attempt. Of these, 43% discussed suicide, underscoring the importance for clinicians of involving family and significant others in treatment. The rate at which persons who made near-lethal attempts sought help from professionals was less than from family and friends. In this study, 37% sought help from a professional, and of these 41% discussed suicide, suggesting the need for improved intervention by professionals.

1.6   Comorbidities

The most significant comorbidities impacting suicide risk are comorbid depression and substance abuse. Each is its own independent risk factor for suicide. Depression and hopelessness have been found to be strongly correlated with death by suicide (Beck, Brown, & Steer, 1989). Of deaths by suicide, 37% have been found to have alcohol present at the time of death (Cherpitel, Borges, & Wilcox, 2004). The presence of substance abuse also makes it more difficult to accept patients' statements that they are not going to attempt to kill themselves. A patient may be able to assure us they are not suicidal when they are sober, but the lack of suicidal ideation or intent while sober may be a poor predictor of the likelihood of suicidal behavior when intoxicated.

Lack of suicidal ideation or intent while sober may be a poor predictor of suicidal behavior when intoxicated

The Institute of Medicine (2002) estimated that about one fourth of all the suicides in the U.S. are individuals with alcohol use disorders (Goldsmith et al., 2002). Without question, more research has been done on the relationship of alcohol to suicidal behavior than any other drug.

In a rigorous review of published studies that evaluated acute alcohol use at the time of death by suicide, Cherpitel et al. (2004) found that toxicology screening and blood alcohol concentration measurements averaged 37% for acute alcohol use. In 16 studies of suicide attempts and acute alcohol use, most of which were conducted in hospital EDs, an average of 40% had acute alcohol use (Cherpitel et al., 2004). Thus for both death by suicide and suicide attempts, acute alcohol use played a role in over one third of the cases, a finding of great clinical significance.

There are several possible mechanisms by which acute alcohol use might make suicidal behavior more likely. A state of intoxication may trigger self-inflicted injuries by intensifying depressive thoughts or feelings of hopelessness while simultaneously lessening inhibitions to hurting oneself (Skog, 1991). There have been efforts to study the relationship more systematically than is possible in simple cross-sectional designs by using a case-crossover study design. Data obtained in this manner has suggested that any acute alcohol use increases the risk of suicide attempts, not only alcohol use that exceeds the legal limits for intoxication. (Cherpitel et al., 2004)

Binge drinking episodes have been found to frequently precede serious suicide attempts (Moscicki, 2001) and death by suicide. While binge drinking has a proximal effect on suicidal behavior, general alcohol consumption had a significant impact over time. Level of general alcohol use predicted suicidal ideation, suicidal communications, and suicide attempts, even when depression and past suicidal behavior were controlled for.

On the basis of an empirical review of cohort studies, Inskip, Harris, and Barraclough (1998) estimated that 7% of alcoholics die by suicide, as compared to their estimate that 6% of those with affective disorders kill themselves. Connor and Duberstein (2004), analyzing retrospective, post mortem studies, found that 34–56% met criteria for alcohol abuse or dependence. Connor and Duberstein (2004) have also examined predisposing and precipitating factors for suicide among alcoholics and attempted a conceptual integration to help inform future research, clinical interventions, and prevention efforts. They propose that aggression/impulsivity, alcoholism severity, and hopelessness are predisposing factors that distinguish alcoholics who are at heightened risk for suicide (see Table 6). Suicide among alcoholics frequently takes place within the context of a major depression and interpersonal stressors, which play some role for suicide in general, but likely play a particularly important role for suicide among alcoholics, particularly partner disruptions.

Alcoholism and depression are frequently comorbid. Postmortem case control studies have shown that rates of depression are higher in alcoholics who died by suicide compared to control groups of alcoholic and substance use disorders (Connor, Beautrais & Conwell, 2003a). Studies have shown major depression to be present at the end of life for suicide decedents with alcohol and substance use disorders in the range of 45% (Connor, Duberstein, & Conwell, 1999) to over 70% (Cheng, 1995). .However, the elevated rate of suicide among alcoholics is not simply due to the elevated base rate of depression in this population (Connor & Duberstein, 2004).

The temporal relationship between alcoholism and depression and the nature of their relationship in death by suicide is not entirely clear (Connor & Duberstein, 2004). In some studies, alcoholism was found to precede depression in adults (Cheng, 1995; Murphy, Armstrong, Hermele, Fischer, & Clendenin, 1979), while a case control study of suicide in adolescents reached the opposite conclusion. In their study of youths, Brent at al. (1993a) found that depression was more likely to precede substance abuse. There may well

> **Binge drinking episodes can frequently precede serious suicide attempts**

Table 6
Risk Factors for Suicidal Behavior Among Alcoholics

Aggression/impulsivity

Alcoholism severity

Hopelessness

Negative affect/episode of major depression

Partner-relationship disruptions

be a sex difference in this regard, at least among adults. While studies such as that of Murphy and Robbins (1967) found alcoholism preceding depression in males, depression is more likely to precede alcoholism among females who die by suicide (Pirkola et al., 1999), a finding consistent with studies that show a general trend for depression to be more likely to precede alcoholism in women than in men (Schuckit et al., 1997).

A general tendency to experience negative affect has been demonstrated to precede the development of major depression, the recurrence of depression and the persistence of depressive symptoms, and is associated with depression in treated substance abusers (Connor & Duberstein, 2004). There may be a subgroup of alcoholics whose depression precedes their alcoholism, and whose drinking is an attempt to cope with their negative affect, who may be at heightened risk of suicide compared to other alcoholics (Preuss et al., 2002).

Partner-related disruptions may be especially important in suicides by those with alcohol and substance abuse disorders

Partner-related disruptions may be particularly important in suicide in alcoholics (Connor & Duberstein, 2004). This finding was first demonstrated in the groundbreaking study of Murphy and Robbin (1967) that showed disruptions in interpersonal relationships occurred more frequently among alcoholics who died by suicide than among any other diagnostic group. A recent case control investigation comparing alcoholics who died by suicide and alcoholic community controls showed that both partner-relationship disruptions and other interpersonal difficulties, including difficulties with other family members, were independent risk factors for suicide (Connor et al., 2003). Similarly, a controlled postmortem study in adolescents who died by suicide found that interpersonal loss, most frequently a break up with a boyfriend or girlfriend, was more common in youths with substance abuse disorders than in youths with mood or conduct disorders who also died by suicide ((Brent et al., 1993b). Connor and Duberstein (2004) make a point that is of particular importance for clinicians: "The proximity of interpersonal disruptions to suicide also hints at their importance, as they tend to cluster in the last six weeks of life in individuals with alcohol or substance abuse disorders." (p. 11).

Aggression and impulsivity may be linked to alcoholism severity. Connor and Duberstein (2004) propose a model that utilizes the construct of reactive aggression. Reactive aggression refers to impulsive, angry responses to aversive events. With more chronic alcohol use patterns, relationships may become more conflictual, with the alcohol use itself a significant source of conflict. More aversive interactions lead to increased impulsive, angry responses. Such individuals may display a pattern of emotional dysregulation and be prone to distressing, interpersonal situations, including inadvertently eliciting rejection by others. Thus, emotional dysregulation, particularly relationship damaging outbursts of anger or hostility, cause interpersonal turmoil and exacerbate depression and hopelessness, intensifying suicide risk.

While far more research has examined the role of alcohol in suicidal behavior than any other drug, emerging information from the National Violent Death Reporting System (Karch, Barker, & Strine, 2006) demonstrated that a variety of different drugs were present at the time of suicide. While 33.3% of suicide decedents tested positive for alcohol, 16.4% tested positive for opiates, 9.4% tested positive for cocaine, 7.7% tested positive for marijuana, and 3.9% tested positive for amphetamines.

In addition to substance abuse comorbidity, the relationship between sui-cidal behavior and trauma is an important, emerging area. The Institute of Medicine (IOM) report emphasized the role of trauma in the development of suicidality. The most comprehensive, longitudinal study of pathways to suicide was conducted in New Zealand and followed 1,265 adolescents. The study found that child sexual abuse, parental alcoholism, and poor attachment to parents were predictive of suicide attempts by age 21, with much of the relationship mediated by mental illness and stressful life events (Fergusson, Woodward, & Horwood, 2000). However, in the National Comorbidity Study, Molnar, Buka, and Kessler (2001) found that while the majority of suicide attempts were attributable to mental disorder, a significant number of suicide attempts occurred in the absence of psychopathology. The IOM report also concluded that sexual abuse was the strongest and most important risk factor for suicide attempts, accounting for 9–20% of all suicide attempts (Goldsmith et al., 2002). Beautrais (2004) found childhood adversity closely linked to repeated suicidal behavior, although not with death by suicide. In the U.S., the Adverse Childhood Experiences Study also documented a powerful, graded effect of childhood trauma on suicide attempts throughout the lifespan (Dube et al., 2001).

1.7   Assessment Procedures

Assessing the risk of suicide is a critical responsibility for clinicians. Since suicide cannot be predicted, making an assessment of risk based on available information is the expected standard of care. Failure to assess risk is an egre-gious professional error by the therapist (Berman, Jobes, & Silverman, 2006). Suicide risk assessment requires careful questioning while maintaining rap-port with the patient. This is more challenging than is commonly understood. Patients are often not asked about suicide, even by experienced clinician's. (Bongar, Maris, Berman, & Litman, 1998). It is important to ask about suicide in a manner that can be experienced as part of a caring conversation. Asking about suicide can sometimes be accompanied by anxiety on the part of the clinician, and lead to questioning in a rote or stiff manner, and patients can frequently sense the clinician's discomfort. Clinician's must be sufficiently comfortable with doing suicide risk assessments that they can ask the nec-essary questions to get the information they need to estimate risk. Ideally, patients will experience this as a deepening of the therapeutic conversation, rather than as a detour or distraction from what they feel they really need to talk about.

There is no one standard way to ask the question about suicide, nor one standard time in a session that the question be asked. What is important is that the question be clear, direct, and specific. Terms like "hurting yourself" or "harming yourself" should be avoided. At times, suicide can be asked about as part of a two-step inquiry. For example, asking first about hopelessness and then about suicide, or first about the wish to be dead and then about suicide. However, even if hopelessness or the wish to be dead are denied, the question about suicide should still be asked.

Suicide cannot be predicted, so risk assessment based on the available information is the expected standard of care

Clinical Pearl
Examples of Questions about Suicide

- Are you thinking about suicide?
- Are you thinking about killing yourself?
- Are you thinking about ending your life?
- Do you ever feel hopeless? Have you ever felt so hopeless that you wanted to kill yourself?
- Do you ever wish you were dead? When you have wished you were dead, did you ever think of suicide?

The simple denial of suicidal ideation is insufficient evidence to determine an absence of suicide risk

The simple denial of suicidal ideation is insufficient evidence to determine an absence of suicide risk. One recent study of 76 suicides that occurred during inpatient hospitalization or immediately after discharge reported that 78% of the patients had denied suicidal ideation when last assessed (Busch, Fawcett, & Jacobs, 2003). While some of these denials may have been truthful, many patients may have concealed their suicidal thoughts; either because they were already planning their death and did not want to be stopped, or because they did not want to be forced to remain in the hospital. This underscores the importance of mastering the art of eliciting information about suicidal ideation. Emphasizing that talking about suicidal thoughts with your therapist does not

Clinical Vignette
Probing for Suicidal Ideation

Bob was attending his first outpatient appointment after being discharged from an inpatient psychiatric unit following a suicide attempt. His therapist asked him if he had any suicidal thoughts since he was discharged four days previously. Bob, hesitated for a moment, and then said "no." His therapist, noticing the hesitation told Bob that continuing to have suicidal thoughts did not mean he would be forced back into the hospital. The therapist explained that he frequently treated people with suicidal thoughts in outpatient therapy, and that therapy was most likely to be helpful if he could talk openly about his suicidal thoughts and what led him to have those thoughts. The therapist further explained that he would only intervene against Bob's wishes if he was convinced that Bob was planning on killing himself within the next several days and was unwilling to work to keep himself safe. Bob then acknowledged that he had thought about suicide two days ago when his daughter had yelled at him after he had punished her for coming in after curfew. The suicidal thoughts were transient, and had not recurred since the argument. Further, Bob's rifle had been taken out of the home by his brother during the inpatient hospitalization. Bob stated, "With the gun gone, I don't even know how I would kill myself." They explored what made the interaction with his daughter so painful he had thoughts about suicide and at the end of the session they invited Bob's wife into the session and discussed that it was likely that Bob would have some suicidal thoughts from time to time. The therapist encouraged Bob both to let his wife know if he was having these thoughts as well as to contact the therapist and gave both of them instructions about how to contact the therapist after hours, as well as the number for the local psychiatric emergency service.

mean automatic, involuntary hospitalization is extremely important and can help provide a greater sense of safety and control for the patient.

Because of potential reluctance to disclose suicidal thoughts, it is important for clinicians to be attuned to nonverbal cues when talking about suicide. A delayed response, reluctance to make eye contact, a sigh or a moment's agitation, could all be signs that suicidal thoughts are present. Additional promising techniques for eliciting suicidal ideation have been developed by Shawn Shea. In a guide from 2002, he describes the importance of "validity techniques," approaches to interviewing that can be used to ask about a variety of issues that are often concealed, such as substance abuse or domestic violence, as well as for inquiries about suicide. Examples of these techniques include the behavioral incident, where questions are focused on obtaining descriptions of behavior rather than obtaining opinions, for example, "What did you drink yesterday?" rather than "Do you have a drinking problem?" Likewise, "Just before you took the 12 aspirin, what thoughts were going through your mind?" is superior to "When you took the pills, do you think you were really trying to kill yourself?" Other examples of validity techniques include "shame attenuation," "gentle assumption," and "normalization." An example of normalization would be, "People who feel depressed and hopeless frequently think about suicide. Have you ever had thoughts about ending your life?"

Once a patient has acknowledged suicidal ideation, it is very important to get additional information about the person's suicidal thoughts. Suicidal thoughts can vary in frequency and in intensity. They may be experienced as intrusive and difficult to ignore or transitory and easier to dismiss. It is also important to understand what has led to the thoughts and the consequences of having these thoughts. Suicidal thoughts may be triggered by certain contexts, such as an argument with someone, and for many persons with chronic suicidal ideation, their suicidal thoughts function as escape behavior, an automatic response to intense emotional pain. It is especially important to remember

Clinicians should to be attuned to nonverbal cues when talking about suicide

---

Clinical Pearl
Additional Questions About Suicide

- How often do you think of killing yourself?

- When did the suicidal thoughts start?

- How long do the thoughts last?

- How intense are the thoughts?

- Do you tell anyone about the thoughts? How did they respond?

- After you started to think about suicide, did you do anything to act on the thoughts?

- Did you think about how you would kill yourself?

- Do you have a firearm available to you?

- Have you ever made a suicide attempt?

- (If the patient reports he or she has not made a suicide attempt) What is the closest you have come to acting on your suicidal thoughts?

that suicidal thoughts are typically connected to the patient's deepest pain. By attempting to understand a patient's suicidal thoughts we are simultaneously trying to understand what most distresses them, what they experience as most intolerable, and why. Ultimately, a suicide risk assessment should be part of a caring conversation in which the therapist is practiced enough in assessing risk that the patient should experience no discordance between their telling of their story and the therapist's assessment of risk.

There is a long history in suicidology of searching for reliable and valid suicide assessment instruments that can inform the clinical assessment of suicide risk (Rogers & Oney, 2005). Prediction of death by suicide was probably never a feasible goal, so attention has turned instead to assessment of risk, rather than prediction. Range and Knott (1997) published a review of 20 suicide assessment instruments, including scales that relied upon clinician rating, self rating, those assessing buffers against suicide, measures for adolescents and children, and more specialized instruments. Based on their review of the existing reliability and validity data, and their ease of administration in clinical settings, Range and Knott (1997) recommended the Beck Scale for Suicidal Ideation (Beck, Kovacs, & Weissman, 1979), the Reasons for Living Inventory (Linehan, Goodstein, Nielsen, & Chiles, 1983), and the four-item version of Linehan's (1981) Suicide Behaviors Questionnaire.

Despite these extensive efforts, survey information regarding how clinicians actually assess risk in real world settings found that clinicians rarely use suicide specific risk assessment tools (Jobes, Eyeman, & Yufit, 1995). In attempting to understand the reasons for this, Jobes (2006) concluded that clinicians tended to pervasively rely on the clinical interview and perceived suicide risk assessment tools as impractical and without clear treatment or management implications. There was also a perception that such instrument failed to capture essential but elusive aspects of suicidality (Jobes, 2006).

Clinical use of such instruments must always be as a component of a more thorough suicide risk assessment utilizing a clinical interview. However, the combination of interview and assessment instruments does have much to recommend it. By utilizing both, consistency between responses can be explored. The relationship context is very important to understand with regard to the use of assessment instruments. For some, suicidality may be more likely to be disclosed on self-report forms than in an interview, particularly when the interviewer is a stranger. There may be a particular utility in combining interview and assessment instruments upon intake or initial interview, when there is not yet an existing, collaborative relationship. The use of an instrument that focuses on the client's wish to die, combined with an instrument like Linehan's that focuses on reasons for living, may be particularly important, as only by doing so can we fully appreciate the client's ambivalence about suicide, both the wish to die and the desire to live.

Combining clinical interview with assessment instruments is recommended

Rogers and Oney (2005) emphasize the importance of the relationship context in suicide risk assessment. Clinician's may respond to concerns about suicide by becoming pre-occupied with assessing risk, and this can lead to not paying sufficient attention to the therapeutic relationship. Being asked endless questions about suicidality can lead to a disconnection with patients, especially if they feel there is no engagement with their pain but rather a focus on the therapist's own anxiety and concerns about liability. Supplementing the interview with assessment instruments can thus help meet the therapist's need for additional information without overwhelming patients with too many questions that are disconnected from the pain driving them toward suicide or the buffers keeping them alive.

Rogers and Oney (2005) point out that the Suicide Status Form devised by David Jobes as part of the Collaborative Assessment and Management of Suicidality (CAMS; Jobes, 2006) includes an explicit focus on collaborative assessment. The Suicide Status Form is part of an overall process of clinical assessment, treatment planning, and management of suicidal risk for suicidal outpatients that has collaboration at its core. The Suicide Status Form is used within the CAMS approach to conduct an initial, multidimensional assessment of suicide risk, develop a suicide-specific treatment plan, track and document ongoing suicidal risk, and determine and document clinical outcomes. Jobes' system is an example of the important connections between initial risk assessment, treatment planning, ongoing monitoring of suicidal risk, and documentation of outcomes.

The Columbia Suicide Severity Rating Scale (Posner et al., 2007) is a newly developed instrument that also shows significant promise for clinical use.

2

Theories and Models of Suicidal Behavior

2.1   Neuropsychiatric Theories

Neuropsychiatric theories of suicide emphasize the genetic and biomedical vulnerabilities associated with these tragic deaths. An important method for estimating the contribution of genetics to suicide are twin studies, which compare the concordance of death by suicide among identical twins, who share the same genetic material, to fraternal twins, who do not. In a review of twin studies of deaths by suicide, Roy, Rylander, and Sarchiapone (1997) found that out of 129 identical twin pairs, when one twin died by suicide, the other twin died by suicide 17 times. In contrast, out of 270 nonidentical twin pairs, the other twin died by suicide only twice. This difference provides strong evidence for the important contribution of genetics to suicide. Additional evidence comes from adoption studies in which the rate of suicide among biological relatives of adoptees was found to be higher than among the adopted families (Shulsinger, Kety, Rosenthal, & Wender, 1979). However, as Jamison (1999) points out, the concordance rate of 15%, while supporting a genetic contribution, also demonstrates that psychological and environmental factors have a clear role. In fact, the concordance rate for suicide is actually less than for severe mental illnesses such as manic-depression and schizophrenia (Jamison, 1999).

The genetic contribution to suicide presumably acts by creating a biological vulnerability, which then interacts with environmental factors to intensify

The association between suicide risk and low levels of CSF 5-HIAAA has often been found

risk. A frequently replicated finding is the association between suicide risk and low levels of CSF 5-HIAAA, a metabolite of serotonin (Jamison, 1999). Persons with mood disorders who attempted suicide and who had low levels of this serotonin metabolite were more likely to die by suicide within a year than those with higher levels (Asberg, 1997). Post mortem studies have also found serotonin abnormalities in the prefrontal cortex of the brain (Stanley & Stanley, 1989), which could be associated with disinhibition or impulsivity. The potential role of the serotonin system in suicidal behavior is important for two other reasons: Early adverse events have been shown to impact the serotonergic system and with the widespread use of a new generation of anti-depressants, the selective serotonin reuptake inhibitors (SSRIs), there was hope that these medications could reduce suicide (Goldsmith et al., 2002). While these medications are demonstrably effective as treatments for depression, their effectiveness in preventing suicide is still uncertain.

Most mental health professionals believe suicide results from complications of untreated mental disorders, and that suicide reflects the severity of those disorders. For example, a person with untreated major depression that does not remit may eventually become hopeless and suicidal. Indeed, psychological autopsy studies, which use multiple informants to delve deeply into the lives of those who have died by suicide, have consistently shown that in the U.S. over 90% of suicide deaths are associated with diagnosable mental disorder (Goldsmith et al., 2002).

> **Over 90% of suicide deaths are associated with diagnosable mental disorder**

However, while acknowledging the link between mental illness and suicide, the Institute of Medicine (IOM), in its landmark summary of the field entitled *Reducing Suicide: A National Imperative*, emphasized that in some cultures, such as China, there is not a prominent link between mental illness and suicide (Goldsmith et al., 2002). In addition, the fact that the majority of those even with the types of mental illness most associated with suicide, such as depression or substance abuse, do not die by suicide underscores the complex biopsychosocial nature of suicide and makes it difficult to conceptualize suicide as solely a complication of mental disorders or as a behavior that simply reflects an exacerbation of a mental disorder. Best estimates are that suicide rates among those who had previously been treated for a depressive disorder as inpatients are about twice as high (4.1%) as the rates for those who had been treated as outpatients (2%). Those treated as inpatients following suicide ideation or suicide attempts, are about three times as likely to die by suicide (6%) as those who were only treated as outpatients (Bostwick & Pancratz, 2000). Together these results suggest there may be a hierarchy of risk based on a patient's treatment history. Yet even among this high risk group, the vast majority do not die by suicide.

2.2   Psychological Theories

The question of why people kill themselves has been asked for millennia, but psychological science has only been meaningfully brought to bear on this critical question over the last half-century.

Several psychological theories have made important contributions to our understanding of suicide. While the link between mental illness and suicide is clear, the majority of those with depression or substance abuse as risk factors do not die by suicide. While comorbidity further increases the risk, this is still not a sufficient explanation for why the majority of those with these two potent risk factors do not die by suicide.

The first major psychological theory was developed by Edwin Shneidman, the father of suicide prevention in the U.S. Shneidman posited that suicidal behavior had a purpose, and that it is an attempt to escape from unendurable psychological pain. He called this psychological pain "psychache" (Shneidman, 1996). Without this deep psychological pain, there is no suicide. He also described the role of "perturbation," a concept similar to agitation or emotional volatility. Research on the role of anxiety as an acute risk factor for suicide appears to support this concept (Busch et al., 2003). He also was the first to speak systematically about lethality. As Joiner points out (2005), not all those with overwhelming psychological pain will engage in lethal self-destructiveness.

Shneidman proposed ten commonalities of suicide (see Table 7). For, example he proposed that cognitive constriction was a common characteristic

Suicidal people often have tunnel vision and see no alternative solution to suicide

of the suicidal individual. Suicidal people have "tunnel vision" and don't see alternatives to suicide as solutions for ending their pain. He also believed the most common emotions in suicide were hopelessness and helplessness

Shneidman was also the first to emphasize that suicidal individuals are typically ambivalent about dying. This ambivalence can continue right up until the moment of death. Anecdotes from some who have survived jumping off the Golden Gate Bridge describe how moments after jumping these individuals regretted their action. Similarly, it is not uncommon in clinical practice to encounter individuals who have called a hotline or ambulance after taking an overdose. This is at times misinterpreted as meaning the suicide attempt was not "serious." However, this behavior is best interpreted as a manifestation of the ambivalence that is so common among suicidal persons.

Ambivalence about suicide can continue right up until the moment of death

Building on the foundation of psychological theory laid down by Shneidman, other theorists have made additional important contributions. For example, cognitive behavioral theories have made major contributions to the understanding of suicide; two salient examples include Aaron Beck and Marsha Linehan. Beck emphasized the significant role of hopelessness as a risk factor. He provided the research that confirmed Shneidman's initial observations. In a study of 207 patients hospitalized for suicidal ideation, only hopelessness predicted the 14 who died by suicide over the next decade (Beck, Steer, Kovaks, & Garrison, 1985). Beck also posited the role of cognitive sensitization. Over time, with repetition, suicide-related thoughts or behaviors become favored (Beck, 1996), Additional research has explored other significant cognitive variables first identified by Shneidman that may constitute core components of suicidality. What makes a person view their situation as unendurable? What drives the compulsion to act? And what determines the sense that there are no other options than suicide? One important line of research has focused on "overgeneral memory," a form of autobiographical memory that focuses on a person's life history (Williams, Barnhofer, Crane, & Dugan, 2006). Suicidal persons tend to not remember events in their personal history in specific detail. Instead, these events are recalled generally and the memories are colored by the person's depression and hopelessness.

Table 7
Shneidman's 10 Commonalities of Suicide

- The common purpose of suicide is to seek a solution.
- The common goal of suicide is cessation of consciousness.
- The common stimulus for suicide is unbearable psychological pain.
- The common stressor in suicide is frustrated psychological needs.
- The common emotion in suicide is hopelessness-helplessness.
- The common cognitive state in suicide is ambivalence.
- The common perceptual state in suicide is constriction.
- The common action in suicide is escape.
- The common interpersonal act in suicide is communication of intention.
- The common pattern in suicide is consistency of lifelong styles.

Reprinted from Shneidman, E. S. (1996). *The suicidal mind*. New York: Oxford University Press, by permission of Oxford University Press, Inc.

Williams also points out that different general pathways may exist for suicidal behavior. One pathway is believed to be driven by hopelessness while the other is strongly related to failures in affect regulation. In hopelessness driven suicide, a sense of entrapment would escalate to suicidality through repeated failures in solving problems and resulting hopelessness. Affect driven suicidal behavior may result from a fundamental failure of affect regulation and the intrusion of distressing memories.

One can differentiate between hopelessness driven and affect driven suicidal behavior

Linehan (1993) has developed the most significant scientific analysis of the role of emotion in suicidal behavior. Her theory and treatment for chronically suicidal women grew out of her experiences with clients who met the diagnostic criteria for borderline personality disorder. Using the most recent understandings of the science of emotion and embedding her work within a functional analytic perspective, she has added a powerful, new dimension to empirically informed treatments for suicidal behavior. Emotional dysregulation is a key concept in Linehan's model. Chronically suicidal persons frequently experience strong emotions; they respond emotionally to a wide variety of cues and their responses are intense. They have difficulty tolerating this emotional distress without resorting to behaviors that help them escape or moderate these intense and painful emotions. Linehan also describes the complex behavioral chains that often exist, including emotions triggering other emotions, such as anger triggering guilt, or shame triggering anxiety. Her approach has also focused on suicidal behavior and its functions. Suicidal behavior can be either operant or respondent; it can be reinforced by its consequences or it can be a direct response to a stimulus. Suicidal behavior will frequently function as escape behavior, as noted by Shneidman. Not only is the ultimate aim of suicidal behavior frequently an escape from emotional pain, but the very act of self-harm and self-injury can function as an escape from emotional pain, insofar as the attention of the person making the attempt becomes focused on the attempt itself rather than the emotional pain the person is experiencing. Indeed, even suicidal ideation can be negatively reinforced, as the very thought of suicide can function as an escape (albeit only momentary) from pain.

Chronically suicidal persons frequently experience intense emotions in response to a wide variety of cues

While Linehan has focused on the development of suicidal behavior generally, Joiner (2005) has focused on what produces lethal suicidal behavior. Joiner has emphasized that human beings do not easily come to an act of final, lethal, self-destruction. For most of us, the fear of death is stronger than any other motivation. Our determination to survive has been developed over hundreds of thousands of years of human evolution. What leads this incredibly powerful behavioral tendency in people to not only be overcome but reversed, so that a person becomes the deliberate agent of his or her own death? Joiner emphasizes that, for this to occur, a capacity to enact lethal self-injury must be learned. Individuals are not born with this capacity for lethal self-injury and pain, and people who die by suicide have to work their way up to it. They must lose their natural fear of death in order to undertake an extreme and difficult form of action. How is this fear reduced? According to Joiner (2005), this occurs through a form of practice involving repeated desensitizing exposure. The most obvious form of such practice is found in suicide attempts, the greatest single predictor of death by suicide. With repeated exposure there is habituation. Not only are cultural or personal taboos against suicide eroded, but the fear of death and the pain associated with suicide attempts gradually diminish-

With repeated exposure, cultural or personal taboos against suicide erode, and the fear of death diminishes

es. One can see in many patients an escalating pattern of increased lethality of suicide attempts (Beautrais, 2004), leading to ultimate death by suicide. In this model, suicidal ideation can also be seen as a form of habituation, as repeated imaginal exposure to the idea of suicide reduces the fear. Joiner theorizes that opponent processes may play a role. Opponent process theory predicts that with repetition, the effects of a provocative stimulus diminish, and the opposite effect, or opponent process, becomes amplified and strengthened.

Joiner (2005) emphasizes that both suicidal desire and suicidal capacity must be present before a suicide occurs. People who die by suicide must both want to kill themselves and be able to kill themselves. Joiner argues that there are those who want to die by suicide but can't, as well as those who can but don't want to (Joiner, 2005). While the concept of lethality has long been an important component of theoretical and clinical work with suicidal people, Joiner's unique contribution has been the recognition that people must acquire the capacity to enact lethal self-injury. The natural and profound inhibitions humans possess against suicide are only overcome through repeated, desensitizing experiences. This desensitizing can take place through suicide attempts, suicidal ideation, witnessing violence and trauma, or other provocative experiences. These are the people who kill themselves, according to Joiner (2005).

Joiner has also emphasized the role of perceived burdensomeness and failed belongingness as suicide risk factors. He views these as critical in determining why a person wants to die by suicide. Building on Shneidman's notion that "psychache," or unendurable psychological pain, is central to suicide, Joiner (2005) argues that those who want to die by suicide are often those who perceive themselves as a burden on others, or who don't perceive themselves as belonging. Many suicidal people no longer regard themselves as effective members of their families or communities, but instead regard themselves as burdens. It is this experience of self as a burden to those one loves that may play a critical role in dying by suicide despite the presence of supportive, caring others. When encountered in psychotherapy, this maladaptive belief system must be vigorously addressed. Failed belonging is related to the painful experience of social isolation.

To summarize Joiner's theory, to die by suicide people must want to kill themselves and be able to kill themselves. Who wants to die by suicide? Those who feel that they are a burden upon others or feel they don't belong. Who is able to die by suicide? Those who have acquired the capacity for lethal self-injury (Joiner, 2005).

Clinical Pearl
Acquiring the Capacity for Lethal Self-Injury

For years, I have heard from many patients who were having suicidal thoughts that they did not believe they had the "courage" to kill themselves. I listened to these statements without quite understanding what I was hearing. Because I did not believe suicide was an act of "courage," having spoken to too many families grievously wounded by a death by suicide, I did not pay sufficient attention to these statements. These patients were telling me they had not yet acquired the capacity for lethal self-injury, although that did not mean they would not acquire this capacity in the future.

3

Risk Assessment and Treatment Planning

Treatment for individuals at risk for suicide must begin with a treatment plan based on a comprehensive suicide risk assessment. This presumes that suicidality was either the reason for treatment or was uncovered during the initial assessment. When suicidality emerges during the course of treatment (i.e., a person with no past history of suicidal behavior makes a suicide attempt or discloses suicidal ideation while in treatment), the treatment plan should be immediately modified to address the suicide risk. This doesn't mean that other issues previously being addressed in therapy need to be dropped, but neither should there be a return to treatment as usual.

Treatment planning for individuals at risk for suicide should always directly target the individual's suicide risk, and include attention to how suicide risk will be assessed, managed, and treated on an on-going basis. Berman et al. (2006) have emphasized that too often clinician's utilize the treatment they are comfortable with rather than directly addressing suicidal behavior.

> **Treatment planning for individuals at risk for suicide should directly target the individual's suicide risk**

Not directly addressing suicidal behavior in the treatment plan is often associated with the view that treating the underlying diagnostic conditions is synonymous with addressing suicidal risk. The clear link between mental illness and suicide has led mental health professionals to assume that by treating the underlying disorder (e.g., depression or substance abuse), suicide risk can be reduced and suicide prevented. However, there is little evidence this is the case (Linehan, 2008). The systematic exclusion of suicidal patients from both medication and psychotherapy trials mean that the efficacy of many treatments for the diagnostic conditions associated with suicide are simply unknown. The implications of this lack of evidence is certainly not that such disorders should go untreated, nor that treating the underlying disorder should not be part of the treatment plan. There is compelling logic for using treatment to modify any risk factors whenever possible. For example, reducing substance abuse clearly is an important goal in the treatment of suicidal persons. The problem is assuming that treating the underlying disorder is sufficient to prevent suicide. It is not, and it is important for therapists to treat the suicidal behavior, thoughts, or desires directly.

This direct attention on suicide risk must be reflected in the treatment plan as well. Not including suicide risk in the treatment plan makes the clinician seem oblivious to the possibility of suicide or suicide attempts. For patients with a past history of suicidal thoughts or behavior, the possibility must be anticipated.

> **Not including suicide risk in the treatment plan makes the clinician seem oblivious to the possibility of suicide or suicide attempts**

Every comprehensive clinical assessment needs to answer several key questions. These include determining the current level of suicide risk (including whether an acute emergency exists that requires emergency intervention)

Clinical Pearl
Treatment Planning with Suicidal Persons

- Identify the pain (psychache)
- Assess risk and protective factors
- Estimate risk level from risk and protective factor information
- Distinguish between acute and chronic risk levels
- Resolve contradictory risk factors
- Determine whether risk and protective factors can be modified
- Target interventions to lower risk or increase protective factors

and obtaining information about risk and protective factors that may need to be addressed in long-term treatment planning. This must be accomplished while maintaining a fluid and collaborative relationship with the patient that allows him to tell his story and explain the pain that is leading him to consider ending his life.

3.1   Assessing Suicide Risk and Protective Factors

The treatment plan should identify both risk and protective factors, estimate risk based on these factors (including how risk may be expected to change over time), determine whether risk and protective factors can be modified, and explain how the treatment plan will attempt to reduce this risk level.

Assessing suicide risk factors should include but not be limited to examining the roles of depression and substance abuse. As Joiner suggests, those who die by suicide will be those who have the desire to, and who have also acquired the capacity to do so. Suicidal ideation is very prevalent among those with major depressive episodes with as many as half of those with major depressive episodes having suicidal ideation, the desire to die (SAMHSA, 2006). Those who abuse substances may be more likely to experience the kind of provocative experiences that will increase the capacity to inflict lethal self-harm.

But in addition to depression and substance abuse, other risk factors must be assessed as well (see Table 8). Social withdrawal, social isolation, and the experience of oneself as a burden to loved ones must be explored. The patient's sense of belonging and the existence of meaningful social connections should be actively assessed and addressed in the treatment plan. Social withdrawal is common in depression, and substance abuse can cause alienating conflict. It is noteworthy that the research of Murphy et al., (1979) on suicide in alcoholics identified interpersonal conflict as a major precipitant. However, neither depression nor substance abuse needs to be present for these risk factors to contribute to increased risk.

Additional risk factors to be assessed include the presence of past suicidal behavior, access to potentially lethal means, including firearms, as well as hopelessness and impulsivity.

Table 8
Risk Factors for Suicide

- Mental disorders, particularly mood disorders, schizophrenia, anxiety disorders, and borderline personality disorder
- Alcohol and other substance use disorders
- Hopelessness
- Impulsiveness and/or aggression
- Trauma and abuse
- Previous suicide attempt (efforts to prevent discovery and regret upon survival convey additional risk)
- Relational or job loss
- Access to lethal means
- Social isolation
- Perceived burdensomeness
- Difficulty asking for help
- Barriers to accessing health care, particularly behavioral health care

Assessing for protective factors is a critical, but sometimes neglected part of the suicide risk assessment as well. At times, the protective factors can be the mirror image of the risk factors. For example, social isolation is a risk factor, while social connection a protective factor. A history of reaching out for help when in a suicidal crisis is a protective factor; a history of not reaching out for help when in a suicidal crisis is a risk factor. Various cultural and religious beliefs may serve to inhibit acting on suicidal thoughts. However, assumptions cannot be made on the basis of nominal religious affiliations. There must be a discussion in order to learn how a person's spiritual life impacts their suicide risk.

3.2   Estimating Suicide Risk Level

Estimating the level of suicide risk from the risk and protective factor information obtained during the assessment is a complex process. It is useful to combine the initial interview with self-report instruments, such as the Beck scales. Linehan's *Reasons for Living Inventory* (1983) is particularly valuable for assessing protective factors. However, there is no psychometric formula that can tell the clinician precisely how to estimate the level of risk. Despite this, clinicians must take the risk and protective factor information they have and estimate risk based on their own empirically informed clinical judgment This does not mean that estimating suicide risk is purely subjective. It does mean that the science has not yet evolved to a point where we can know with certainty how the empirically supported risk and protective factors combine in individual cases to determine if risk is low, moderate, or high.

Further, suicide risk always has a time dimension. Risk is not static, and it can fluctuate greatly over time. Risk also can be acute or chronic. High, acute risk may require hospitalization, while chronic risk should typically be addressed in outpatient therapy. An understanding of suicidal behavior or a suicidal crisis in the patient's past history can help the clinician anticipate the circumstances under which acute risk might emerge. For example, if a patient has made a suicide attempt after losing a job, and is currently having work-related problems, it can reasonably be anticipated that loss of the current job could lead to thoughts of suicide.

There is no psychometric formula to estimate a client's specific level of risk

Risk monitoring is a critical component of outpatient treatment of suicidal persons. Fluctuations in risk status may necessitate intensification of treatment. Risk must be monitored systematically for patients for whom suicide has been an issue. At minimum, risk must be assessed at critical points in treatment. According to Bongar (2002), risk should be assessed at intake, as well as at transitional points in treatment.

When there is evidence of increased risk, the treatment plan must be changed to respond to this increased risk, or must already include provisions regarding responding to exacerbations in suicide risk levels. During periods of increased risk, risk monitoring should take place during every clinical contact.

3.3   Resolving Contradictory Risk Factors

It is critical to understand that while there is a substantial literature on risk and protective factors, there is no formula for how these factors should be put together to estimate risk for an individual person. While it is reasonable to assume that risk accumulates with each additional risk factor, or is lessened with each additional protective factor, there is no empirically derived calculus for making these critical determinations. Rather, risk and protective factors form a mosaic whose pattern must be discerned. Should each risk factor be weighed equally? That seems unlikely. A history of past near-lethal suicide attempts is more worrisome than living alone. Yet, in certain clinical circumstances, living alone may be a crucial factor. So how are these differing risk factors to be weighed in making an estimation of risk? Systematic risk estimation techniques exist that assign numerical weight to different risk factors, but clinicians have been very reluctant to use them, and their value for aiding near term clinical decision-making has not been established. Even the commonly used categories of low, moderate, or high risk do not have clear empirical anchors, especially when used to estimate risk in the time frames needed by clinicians. Clinicians are frequently called upon to estimate risk in the next few hours, days, or weeks. Clinicians, therefore,

Clinicians must rely on a clinical judgment deeply informed by a knowledge of empirically derived risk and protective factors

must rely on clinical judgment, but on a clinical judgment deeply informed by a knowledge of empirically derived risk and protective factors. In some situations, this will be straightforward. If we receive a telephone call from a patient who is intoxicated and holding a loaded gun and is voicing suicidal intent, a randomized control trial is not necessary to inform us that this person is at high and immediate risk. Yet often the clinical picture is not nearly that clear.

For example, the reported absence of suicidal ideation leads us to assume decreased risk, yet a recent suicide attempt will point us in the direction of increased risk. Which outweighs the other? Consider the following cases, each of which is characterized by the absence of current suicidal ideation and the presence of a recent suicide attempt, but where the estimation of risk is very different because of the presence or absence of additional risk or protective factors.

Clinical Vignettes

The Differential Weighing of Suicide Risk Factors

John is a 42-year-old Caucasian male being evaluated at the request of his wife. He denies thinking about suicide but acknowledges that last night, while intoxicated, he had to be restrained by friends from jumping off a bridge. His wife also reports that he called her on the telephone from the bar where he was drinking with his friends and expressed suicidal thoughts to her, a phone call John does not recall making. John has been drinking nightly. John is assessed to be at high risk for suicide given his alcohol abuse and recent interrupted suicide attempt. It appears highly likely that he will drink and become suicidal again within the next few days. It is recommended that he be hospitalized while efforts are made to secure placement in residential alcohol treatment.2

Robert came to an initial session with his wife. They both reported that two nights ago he had made a suicide attempt by overdose of approximately 15 aspirin after an argument with his wife. She had threatened to leave him if he did not get help for "his problems," which included mishandling of money, not spending time with the children, and anger control. Following his suicide attempt, Robert agreed to come to therapy and his wife agreed to not leave him as long as he was "working on his problems." He does not report any suicidal thoughts currently. He appears to be at low risk for suicide at the present time, given the absence of suicidal ideation and the apparent stabilization in the marital relationship.

These two clinical vignettes illustrate how it is the overall patterning of risk and protective factors, rather than the presence or absence of specific risk and protective factors, that must determine our estimation of suicide risk levels. How much weight the clinician will give each risk and protective factor in assessing suicide risk is the essence of clinical judgment when dealing with suicidal patients.

3.4 Understanding the Time Dimension of Suicide Risk

Suicide risk is not static, and it fluctuates over time. Someone may be at low risk today, but at very high risk in the future.

In clinical practice, we are most often concerned with the patient's current level of suicide risk. When a patient leaves our office after a weekly appointment, our most basic concern is whether they will be back next week. Yet understanding whether a patient is at imminent risk is much more art than

Clinical Vignette
Suicide Risk Fluctuates Over Time

James is a 55-year-old Irish-American male. He had experienced a series of devastatingly painful major depressive episodes. He had made a series of suicide attempts of escalating lethality. His most recent suicide attempt would have been fatal if not for his unexpectedly having been found by a case worker dropping by to check on him. James was quite clear that he would rather kill himself than endure another major depression. However, he had no present plans to kill himself. While he experienced depressed mood as part of the dysthymic disorder that consistently was with him, he could endure this. What he could not tolerate was the intensified pain of the next major depressive episode he anticipated would come in the future. Given the absence of present suicidal ideation or intent, his suicide risk at the time of assessment was low, but his suicide risk in the future was extremely high. He will need to be carefully monitored as any intensification of depression could lead to escalating suicide risk requiring acute intervention.

science. Despite the fact that virtually every state incorporates imminent risk (or a similar concept} into its involuntary commitment standards, there is little scientific evidence that clinician's can assess imminent risk in a meaningful way (Simon, 2006). Much of the suicide literature has focused on static risk factors that cannot be considered true warning signs for suicide. Examples include demographic variables such as age or gender that cannot be modified. Warning signs of suicide are based on research identifying acute risk of suicide over a period of months, rather than a period of days or hours that clinicians must utilize to make decisions about issues such as hospitalization.

Suicidal risk is not static; risk can fluctuate greatly over time. Both patients and families need to be educated about the time dimension of suicide risk.

Ultimately, clinicians are responsible for doing the best they can despite the limitations of the research literature. Undoubtedly, in many situations, a clinician's belief that a person was at imminent risk has led to intervention that was lifesaving. Both clinician's and crisis line workers may receive calls from persons who have just made a suicide attempt. Despite the ambivalence expressed by making the call at all, such patients are clearly at imminent risk and typically in need of emergency medical intervention. The person contemplating suicide sitting with a loaded gun right in front of him is clearly at imminent risk. Beyond such clear situations, what constitutes imminent risk is a clinical judgment based on in depth knowledge of suicide and of the patient.

Maintaining awareness of the time dimension of suicide risk is critical in order to recognize the appropriate role of hospitalization. A frequent misperception that patients, their families, and even providers sometimes have is that suicide risk can be eliminated during hospitalization and that patients are discharged only when their suicide risk has been eliminated. In fact, suicide risk can be reduced during the course of a successful psychiatric hospitalization, but it can rarely be eliminated. The period following discharge from hospitalization has been shown to be a high risk time for suicide. Data from England has documented this risk, with most suicides occurring within the first month following discharge (Appleby et al., 1999).

Clinical Vignette
Anticipating Exacerbation of Suicidal Risk

Ronald was a 41-year-old male hospitalized following a suicide attempt by overdose. He suffered from a major depressive episode complicated by alcohol abuse. There was substantial marital disruption. His wife, Jennifer, in a telephone call with the clinician, revealed that following her husband's discharge she planned to tell him that she had decided to divorce him. She reasoned that after his discharge he would be "doing better," and that this was the best time to tell him this difficult news. The clinician encouraged her, if she had made a final decision, to inform her husband now while he was in the hospital where there was support and protection, rather than telling him after discharge when there would likely be an escalation of suicide risk with far less opportunity for clinical intervention.

3.5   Documenting Suicidal Risk

Documentation of the suicide risk assessment and treatment plan is critical. Many times clinicians do an excellent job of assessing risk and intervening with suicidal individuals, but their documentation does not reflect the high quality of the work they did, leaving the clinician vulnerable to legal liability in the event of a tragic outcome. Gutheil (1990) describes consultation and documentation as the twin pillars of liability prevention. Bongar (2002) emphasizes that an essential element in risk management is the maintenance of timely, meticulous records. Bongar (2002) also points out that every significant decision point in treatment must also include a risk-benefit analysis that describes all actions that were considered, the reasons that led the clinician to make the decision, and the reasons other alternatives were rejected.

It is important to realize that documentation, while critically important for managing risk and preventing liability, is not simply paperwork done to avoid a successful malpractice suit. Please see Table 9 for guidelines for documenting risk. The risk benefit analysis that Bongar (2002) recommends is an extremely important clinical skill for all those working with people at risk for suicide and the documentation of this risk benefit analysis assists the clinician in clearly formulating his or her estimation of risk. Many times, a clinician may have a strong feeling or intuition that a patient is at low or high risk. While it is important for clinicians to respect their own intuitions, it is even more important for the clinician to understand what is influencing that intuition. Skills in risk formulation can be sharpened by the repeated process of articulating how the varying risk and protective factors were differentially weighed, and "thinking out loud for the record" (Gutheil, 1990).

It is important to document the participation of patients, and, if possible, significant others, in the development of the treatment plan, including their understanding of the potential risks and benefits of different treatment decisions, such as whether or not to hospitalize, or to utilize different treatment options such as psychotherapy and medication. Competent patients have a right to be full partners in the decision-making process and their participation should be documented (Bongar, 2002).

Table 9
Guidelines for Documenting Suicide Risk Following A Suicide Attempt or During A Suicidal Crisis

All patients who are evaluated following a suicidal attempt or during a suicidal crisis should have included as part of the documentation of that evaluation a formal assessment of suicidal risk. This should include a specific statement about the overall level of suicidal risk (low, moderate, high) as well as supporting evidence to justify the overall assessment of level of suicidal risk. Relevant factors that should be used in justifying the assessment include, but are not limited to:

- Lethality of recent attempt
- Past suicide attempt history
- Degree of suicidal intent
- Availability of means, including firearms
- Presence of a plan, and degree of planning
- Regret versus relief in response to survival
- Presence of continuing suicidal ideation including frequency and intensity
- Availability of social/family support
- Family history of suicide
- Presence of active psychotic symptoms
- Presence of major depression and/or hopelessness or anhedonia
- Perturbation, anxiety or agitation
- Alcohol/drug involvement
- Impulsivity

Documentation is necessary both at the start of therapy during the initial treatment planning process, as well as on an ongoing basis, with particular attention needed if a suicidal crisis emerges.

Both the presence and absence of the above risk factors should be included in the risk assessment. The level of risk assessed should be meaningfully related to the disposition that is arranged. Since the level of risk can fluctuate on a daily basis, suicidal patients being followed on an out-patient basis should have their level of risk revised or re-affirmed in the documentation of follow-up contacts. Finally for these kinds of cases, obtaining psychiatric and/or supervisory consultation, and documenting this consultation, is of paramount importance.

4

Treatment

While there is substantial evidence that pharmacological treatment of disorders that are risk factors for suicide (such as depression) can be effective, pharmacological studies that have targeted suicide directly have had much more equivocal results. In part, this is because clinical trials of medication have historically excluded those at risk for suicide (as have psychotherapy studies). Evidence for the effectiveness of Lithium in preventing suicide is probably stronger than for any other medication (Cipriani, Pretty, Hawton, & Geddes, 2005). Meltzer (1999) has examined clozapine versus olanzapine for patients with schizophrenia or schizoaffective disorder who were at high risk for suicide and found that those receiving clozapine were less likely to attempt suicide or be hospitalized for suicide risk.

An area of significant controversy recently has been the relationship between the use of SSRIs and suicide risk. While previously the major debate within the field has focused on whether the significantly increased rates of prescription of SSRIs was responsible for a decrease in national suicide rates in various countries around the world (Safer & Zito, 2007), fears about the potential role of SSRIs in causing suicide erupted in England and the United States. This concern about suicidality as a possible side effect from the use of SSRIs led the Food and Drug Administration to issue a "black box" warning. The focus of concern was initially on youths, because the evidence of efficacy for treatment of depression among this group was much more equivocal than the evidence among adults, making the risk/benefit ratio more problematic among youths than adults. Following this warning, prescriptions of SSRIs fell significantly. When the youth suicide rate increased in 2004, after almost a decade of decline, some argued that the decrease in use of SSRIs was to blame. While there may be a subgroup of those who take SSRIs who experience an increase in suicidality (Maris, 2007), this does not mean that they are not safe for most patients, particularly those with serious depression. Gibbons, Brown, Hur, Marcus, Bhaumik, and Mann (2007) report that among male veterans treated with SSRIs, suicide attempts decreased. However, their effectiveness in preventing death by suicide is still uncertain.

A review of the literature by Rudd, Joiner, and Rajab (2001), which focused only on nonpharmacologic interventions, revealed only 25 randomized or controlled studies that targeted suicidality. They divided their review into intervention studies and treatment studies. Intervention studies were those that did not provide any kind of psychotherapy or medication treatment. These studies made changes in either procedures associated with treatment (letters, phone calls), or facilitated access to mental health services and assessed any subsequent reductions in suicide attempts. Of particular note was a study by

Jerome Motto (1976) that found a reduction in death by suicide over a two-year period of patients who refused treatment, who received non-demanding letters compared to those who did not receive such letters. However, the impact was not maintained over the full five years of the study.

The Rudd, Joiner, and Rajab (2001) review of the intervention studies yielded the following conclusions: Intensive follow-up, case management, telephone contacts, letters or home visits may improve treatment compliance over the short-term for lower risk cases. Improved ease of access (i.e., a clearly stated crisis plan) to emergency services can potentially reduce subsequent attempts and service demand by first-time suicide attempters. The conclusions from the Rudd, Joiner, and Rajab (2001) review of treatment studies are summarized in Table 10.

In review studies published following the Rudd, Joiner, and Rajab (2001) summary, the best validated approach for reducing suicidal behavior remains DBT (Linehan, 1993), which has been shown in randomized control studies to reduce suicidal behavior, as well as reduce time spent in the hospital for patients with histories of chronic suicidal behavior. DBT has been shown to be effective both in controlled trials compared to treatment as usual, as well as when compared to expert treatment, as demonstrated in a recently published randomized control trial (Linehan et al., 2006). As such, it is the treatment of choice for those with a history of multiple suicide attempts, particularly those who meet diagnostic criteria for borderline personality disorder Since DBT has been primarily studied and found effective with women who have made multiple suicide attempts, there is a pressing need to research its efficacy with men who make multiple suicide attempts.

Recent research has also shown that short-term treatments can also reduce repeat suicide attempts, at least among those who have made a single suicide attempt. A recent randomized control trial by Greg Brown and colleagues (2005) documented a reduction in suicide attempts. Utilizing a 10-session cognitive therapy intervention designed to prevent repeat suicide attempts in adults who

---

Table 10
Summary of the Rudd, Joiner, & Rajab (2001) Review

Implications for clinical practice from the treatment studies were:

- Intensive, longer term treatment following a suicide attempt is most appropriate and effective for those identified at high risk as indicated by multiple attempts, psychiatric history, and diagnostic comorbidity.

- Short-term CBT, integrating problem solving training as a core intervention, is effective at reducing suicidal ideation, depression, and hopelessness over periods of up to one year. Such brief approaches do not appear effective at reducing attempts over longer time frames.

- Reducing suicide attempts requires longer term treatment modalities targeting specific skill deficits such as emotional regulation, poor distress tolerance (e.g., impulsivity), anger management, and interpersonal assertiveness, as well as other enduring problems such as interpersonal relationships and self-image disturbance (e.g., personality disturbance).

- High risk suicidal patients can be safely and effectively treated on an outpatient basis if acute hospitalization is also available and accessible.

recently attempted suicide (Brown et al., 2005), participants in the cognitive therapy group were 50% less likely to reattempt than those in the usual care group. Reductions in depression and hopelessness were also demonstrated in the cognitive therapy group, although reductions in suicidal ideation were not found.

Similarly, a recent randomized control trial by Slee, Garnefski, van der Leeden, Arensman, & Spinhoven (2008) also found reductions in reoccurrence of suicidal behavior in a group of 15–35 year olds, who had recently engaged in either a suicide attempt or an episode of self-harm without suicidal intent, following 12 sessions of cognitive behavior therapy combined with treatment as usual, when compared to treatment as usual alone. Positive effects on suicidal cognitions, symptoms of depression and anxiety, as well as improved problem solving were found. Among the measures of suicidal cognitions impacted were subscales related to distress tolerance and perceived burdensomeness.

A replication of the Motto (1976) study done by Carter, Clover, Whyte, Dawson, D'Este (2005) used postcards sent as a non-demanding follow-up. They found that among patients seen in emergency departments for self-poisoning, the number of self-poisoning episodes was approximately halved, while the proportion of patients who engaged in self-poisoning did not decrease. This study underscores the potential value of this simple intervention, and highlights the importance of continued follow up efforts.

A significant new study conducted under the auspices of the World Health Organization in five countries found a reduction in deaths by suicide using a brief ED intervention combined with follow up over 18 months (Fleischmann et al., 2008). This is only the second randomized controlled trial ever to show a reduction in deaths by suicide, and, like Motto (1976), involved follow up after an acute episode of suicidality.

Treatment of suicidal behavior can take place in various types of settings or levels of care (i.e., inpatient, outpatient, emergency). Patients are frequently hospitalized in order to provide a secure environment in which the risk of death by suicide can be minimized, although not eliminated (according to the Joint Commission on the Accreditation of Healthcare Organizations, JCAHO, inpatient suicides are one of the most frequent "critical incidents" in the U.S. health care system; JCAHO, 2008). Analyses based on both national and state samples of adolescents who have engaged in nonfatal self harm revealed that approximately 45% of those seen in emergency departments were either hospitalized or transferred for specialized medical care (Vajani et al., 2007). Despite this extensive use of inpatient hospitalization, the research base for inpatient hospitalization for suicidality is surprisingly weak. There are no randomized controlled trials showing a reduction in the number of suicides due to psychiatric hospitalization. In part, this is due to the difficulties in achieving adequate sample size to demonstrate reductions in deaths by suicide that plague all suicide research, as well as the systematic exclusion of those at risk for suicide from treatment studies. In addition, those few studies that examined inpatient admission versus a control treatment condition did not demonstrate reductions in self-inflicted injury (Van der Sande et al., 1997; Waterhouse & Platt, 1990). Still, inpatient hospitalization is widely and understandably considered to be an essential component of the continuum of care for suicidal individuals (APA 2003). Inpatient hospitalization, while essential and life saving for some patients at some points, should not be considered the sine qua non for the treatment of suicidal individuals. In particular, reliance on hospitalization as a single, stand alone intervention can be problematic, as suicide risk can rarely be completely eliminated based on a single hospitalization. Hospitalization is not an adequate substitute for a comprehensive continuum of care.

Beautrais (2004) states that the major clinical implications of her studies of mortality and morbidity following a suicide attempt is the need for more intensive and extensive follow-up of those making a suicide attempt. In her further analysis (Gibbs, Beautrais, & Fergusson, 2004), which looked at all hospitalized suicide attempters, she and her co-authors note, "Since a high risk group within the population of those making suicide attempts cannot be reliably identified, intervention strategies should be targeted at all individuals admitted to hospital for attempted suicide." These authors further recommend that since the risk of further attempts and death is greatest in the first two years, support and monitoring should be concentrated during this period. However, the risk remains high 10 years after an index attempt, also indicating a need for longer term support and management.

The standard of care for treatment of suicidal persons does not mandate a specific setting for treatment, such as inpatient hospitalization, nor a specific type of treatment, such as medication or psychotherapy. Rather the standard of care is that clinicians will assess the risk for suicide and implement a treatment plan that is meaningfully linked to the level of risk assessed (Bongar, 2002). While some of the methods and techniques that are described in the pages to come can be utilized in a variety of treatment settings (i.e., inpatient, partial care, outpatient), the primary focus is upon their use in outpatient settings.

4.1   Methods of Treatment

4.1.1   Multiphase Models

Both Linehan (1993) and Rudd, Joiner, and Rajab (2001) recommend the use of multiphase models for the treatment of suicidal behavior. While they use different terminology, the concepts are quite similar. Linehan's first phase of treatment (1993) directly targets suicidal behavior. Whenever suicidal behavior exists, it must be prioritized first, as suicidal behavior not only brings the risk of death, it makes a life worth living impossible. As long as suicidal behavior takes place, it must be the primary target of therapy. Similarly, for Rudd et al. (2001) the initial phase of treatment is symptom management, which has the goals of resolving crises, reducing suicidality, instilling hope, and reducing overall symptomology.

4.1.2   Orientation and Engagement

The start of treatment is perhaps the most important time in therapy. If persons at risk for suicide do not remain in treatment, then treatment can do nothing for them. Yet, there are multiple crucial tasks that must be performed at the start of therapy. These tasks include orienting to treatment, obtaining informed consent, performing a comprehensive suicide risk assessment, connecting with the client, helping him or her to feel understood and able to tell his or her story, and working collaboratively to develop a treatment plan the client feels has the potential to meet his or her needs, including a safety plan to assist in enhancing immediate safety.

Not assessing suicidal risk <u>and</u> substituting assessment for engagement are both clinical errors

While not assessing for suicidal risk is one type of clinical error, substituting assessment for the basic therapeutic task of establishing a relationship is another type of error, one that may be particularly problematic for patients within the health or mental health system who may experience multiple, rote assessments before actually being able to speak to someone who will listen to them. It is not surprising that there is often poor continuity of care and early drop out from treatment if a person in crisis has reached out for help and has had to be seen in multiple settings, or speak to multiple people before they can tell their story and feel connected to another human being who has the potential to help them.

These issues have been addressed by Jobes (2006), Linehan (1993), and others. Jobes (2006) emphasizes the need for an initial, collaborative treatment planning session. To reduce the interpersonal distance, he sits side by side with the client during the process. Linehan also emphasizes the need to establish a strong positive relationship. "With a highly suicidal patient, the relationship with the therapist is at times what keeps her alive when all else fails" (1993, p. 98). When a suicidal client does not engage early in treatment, and drops out, it is important for the therapist to reach out and re-connect. Attempts to contact the patient should be routinely made any time a suicidal client drops out of treatment.

Attempts to contact the patient should be routinely made when a suicidal client drops out of treatment

In addition to conducting an initial, comprehensive suicide risk assessment, performing a diagnostic assessment and making any necessary referrals, for example, to a psychiatrist if medication is needed, is an important element of care. In addition, the therapist should have already in place a process for obtaining consultation regarding the patient's care, as consultation and documentation are typically considered the twin pillars of sound risk management when working with suicidal patients. The availability of consultation will allow the clinician to respond most effectively at critical decision-making points in treatment, such as in deciding whether or not to hospitalize a patient. The agreement of a therapist and a consulting psychiatrist or other professional with hospital admitting privileges to maintain a patient in outpatient care may

---

Clinical Pearl
Tasks to complete at start of treatment

- Establish a therapeutic relationship
- Orient to treatment
- Obtain informed consent
- Perform comprehensive suicide risk assessment
- Perform a diagnostic assessment
- Develop a treatment plan
- Create a safety plan

Clinical Vignette

Informed Consent Regarding Emergency Intervention

Michael is a 44-year-old man with a history of multiple suicide attempts and multiple hospitalizations. At the start of treatment with a new therapist, he was encouraged to disclose any suicidal ideation. Michael clearly denied current suicidal ideation but expressed concern that if he expressed suicidal ideation in the future he would be hospitalized, possibly against his will. His therapist told him, "It is very important for our work together that you are able to let me know about your suicidal thoughts. I will not initiate involuntary hospitalization procedures simply because you are having thoughts about suicide, but only if I am convinced that you are intent on killing yourself in the immediate future and you are unable to work with me on alternative ways of keeping you safe."

help prevent hospitalizations driven chiefly by liability concerns, as the consultation documents that outpatient care was seen by two professionals as a viable plan of care.

Orientating the patient to the treatment is an important early goal of treatment. Discussing goals and expectations, reviewing roles and responsibilities, and obtaining informed consent is sound practice for work with any patient, but it is particularly important when working with suicidal patients. For example, it can be reasonably anticipated that there could be an emergency situation in which breaching confidentiality could become necessary. Such exceptions to confidentiality and the therapist's approach to them should be discussed at the start of therapy. If not, the patient may be surprised and potentially feel betrayed if a breach of confidentiality occurs unexpectedly during the course of treatment. There is little disadvantage to this type of transparency. Clarification that it is not the presence of suicidal ideation by itself, but rather the therapist's judgment that suicide is imminent that would trigger emergency interventions, can be particularly important

> **Patients need a thorough understanding of what treatment will involve to make a realistic commitment to treatment**

Both Rudd et al. (2001) and Linehan (1993) emphasize the importance of this initial orientation to treatment. Rudd states, "It is difficult, if not impossible, for the patient to make a realistic commitment to treatment, without a thorough understanding of just what treatment will involve and what is expected" (p. 81). Informed consent should also routinely include a discussion regarding the potential use of both psychotherapy as well as medication, along with an offer to arrange a psychopharmacology consult if indicated and desired.

Linehan (1993) incorporates having patients agree as a goal of therapy to not kill themselves during the year they are asked to participate in treatment. Linehan's approach should not be confused with a no-suicide "contract." In many cases the therapist can utilize the explicit commitment to the goal at later times during the treatment.

The work of Linehan (1993) and Rudd et al. (2001) highlights the importance of first bringing suicidal behavior under control. As long as there is acute risk, this must be the focus of treatment. This means that the clinician must be familiar with how to manage high risk situations and must also be able to integrate this information into treatment. Yet, bringing suicidal behavior under control, while essential, is not sufficient. A patient who feels miserable and would rather be dead but is not actively suicidal is at significant risk for a resurgence of suicidal behavior. The best suicide prevention is, in Linehan's words, "a life worth living." In this section, we will first look at crisis intervention and management of acute risk and then at treatment to reduce long-term risk.

4.2   Crisis Intervention and the Management of Acute Risk

For the clinician working with patients at risk for suicide, the potential need to manage an acute crisis must be anticipated, and it is essential that the clinician obtain information about both the capabilities and the limitations of the psychiatric emergency system in the communities in which the clinician practices. This should include a clear understanding of what the clinician can provide, as well as the role and limitations of emergency departments (EDs), crisis lines, the police, ambulance and emergency medical technician, and psychiatric emergency services.

Clinical Pearl
Checklist for being prepared for psychiatric emergencies

- Understand your own personal limits
- Determine your phone availability and emergency appointment capacity
- Understand your local psychiatric emergency response system
- Know your ED characteristics (mental health capacity, psychologist privileges)
- Determine your community's mobile outreach capacity
- Know the role, capacities, and limitations of involving the police
- Understand the capacities of local suicide prevention hotlines and crisis centers
- Know how to arrange for a patient at acute and high risk to be voluntarily hospitalized
- Understand involuntary commitment laws

4.2.1   Assuring Telephone Accessibility After Hours

Treating suicidal patients requires availability outside of the psychotherapy session. A patient may experience a suicidal crisis or an intensification of suicidal thoughts or intent at any time, and the clinician must anticipate this possibility. This need for greater availability is one reason many clinicians may be reluctant to take on suicidal patients. Linehan (1993), working with chronically suicidal borderline patients, has made an important contribution by emphasizing that clinician's need to be able to provide telephone consultation, outside of normally scheduled psychotherapy sessions but within the context of personal limits. No clinician can tolerate being on-call 24 hours a day, seven days a week, on an on-going basis. Further, different clinicians will establish different limits. But a clinician must provide suicidal patients with some access

Clinicians working with suicidal patients need to provide telephone availability outside of scheduled sessions

outside of scheduled psychotherapy sessions. A clinician unwilling to provide such accessibility should not treat suicidal patients. Moreover, for those times when the clinician is not available, there must be alternatives. Clinicians must have made defined coverage arrangements (e.g., utilizing other members of a group practice) and must have detailed information regarding the availability and limitations of local emergency departments, psychiatric emergency services, and crisis centers. Further, this information should be routinely conveyed to both the patient and family members/significant others when working with a suicidal patient, so that they are clearly aware of how help can be rapidly accessed in the event of an emergency.

Information on getting help after office hours should be routinely provided to patients and their families

The telephone can be an invaluable tool in the managing the suicidal outpatient (Bongar, 2002). Linehan (1993) has emphasized the importance of telephone availability by the therapist to help suicidal patients use their newfound skills (such as emotional regulation or distress tolerance) as an alternative to suicidal behavior. While there has not yet been a definitive component analysis of DBT to determine the relative role of different components of the DBT treatment package to reduce suicide behaviors, including the role of telephone consultation, it makes sense that phone work would be important. The availability of a clinician who knows you and can prompt and encourage you to engage in alternative behaviors rather than self-destructive behavior may play a key role in skills generalization.

In addition, recent studies of the impact of suicide prevention hotlines have found that distress, hopelessness, and suicidal intent decreased during hotline calls, and distress and hopelessness continued to decline at two-week follow-up. Approximately 13% of callers who agreed to the follow-up spontaneously commented that they felt the call had saved their lives (Gould et al., 2007). If hotline calls to a person unknown to the caller can have this kind of positive impact, then calls with a trusted clinician may achieve similar or better results.

4.2.2   Suicide Prevention Hotlines

The use of crisis lines or suicide prevention hotlines is an important supplement to the clinician's own availability, but does not substitute for the availability of the clinician. Patients must be given clear information about the clinician's availability as well as the availability of other members of the treatment team, and instructions for when a crisis hotline or psychiatric emergency service should be called.

In 2007, the Joint Commission on the Accreditation of Health Care Organizations introduced, for the first time, a national safety goal directly related to suicide prevention. This goal focused on assessing suicide risk. Included as an implementation expectation for this goal was a requirement to provide information such as suicide prevention hotline numbers to those identified as being at risk and their families for use in crisis situations.

Accurate and up-to-date information should be given to patients about local hot lines and crisis centers

The availability of local hotlines and crisis centers varies in different communities, so it is important to acquire information about local resources before giving a patient a hotline number. Some hotlines do not have suicide prevention capacity. For example, in many states and communities there are excellent information and referral services that utilize the 2-1-1 number. While some of these centers are so-called blended centers that can work with suicidal individuals, others do not have this capacity. Crisis centers and their associated local hotline numbers can, and do, go out of business from time to time, yet in the age of the Internet, these numbers can live on via the web. Crisis centers can also vary according to whether they are subject to any kind of licensing or certification. Some may be affiliated with a health care organization and may receive accreditation through the Joint Commission or the Commission on the Accreditation of Rehabilitation Facilities (CARF). The American Association of Suicidology (AAS) also certifies crisis centers and is the only certification that focuses solely on suicide prevention. Others may receive their accreditation through organizations such as the Alliance for Information and Referral Services (AIRS) or Contact USA. Clinicians are advised to contact their local hotline/crisis center directly to determine whether round the clock suicide prevention capacity exists, whether these organizations are certified by a recognized body, and to find out how the clinician and the center can work together constructively.

Clinicians should contact their local crisis services directly to gain information and build relationships

A national suicide prevention hotline number is also available, 1-800-273-TALK, which is funded through SAMHSA and utilizes a national network of crisis centers called the National Suicide Prevention Lifeline. Callers who use the toll fee number 1-800-273-TALK, will be connected to the closest of approximately 130 crisis centers in the U.S.. Crisis centers participating in the network must have appropriate licensing and certification, and must meet network standards in areas such as suicide risk assessment (Joiner et al., 2007). The National Suicide Prevention Lifeline also provides a subnetwork of crisis centers with Spanish language capacity, as well as a veteran's service.

The National Suicide Prevention Lifeline's toll free number, 800-273 TALK, connects the caller with the closest of over 130 crisis centers

4.2.3 Emergency Appointment Capability

In addition to accessibility by telephone, there may be times when it is necessary to schedule an emergency appointment with the patient. This would be indicated in those circumstances in which a telephone contact is not sufficient to reduce risk or assist the patient in coping with suicidal thoughts. The clinician's capacity to provide such appointments will be influenced by the setting in which she or he works, and the immediacy of the patient's need to be seen. For example, a clinician handling a crisis call at night might offer to see a patient the following morning. This requires the clinician to make an assessment, in collaboration with the patient, that the patient can maintain safety until the appointment. In some circumstances, a face-to-face assessment cannot be postponed until the next day, and if this is after office hours are closed, referral to a hospital emergency room may be necessary. For many clinicians, this may mean their patient may need to be assessed by someone who doesn't know them.

In addition to providing an emergency appointment at a time of heightened risk, clinicians should consider increasing the frequency of appointments. Welu (1977) demonstrated a decrease in suicide attempts with intensified treatment in the period/month following a suicide attempt. Potentially, such intensification of appointment frequency may reduce or prevent suicidal behavior.

When responding to increased risk, increase the intensity of treatment

4.2.4   Use of the Emergency Department

When a patient requires emergency department (ED) care, there may still be significant decisions that the clinician needs to make. In some instances, the decision may be straightforward, for example, in the case of a patient who has overdosed where the response will be to call 9-1-1 to dispatch emergency medical personnel. In other instances, decision making may not be as clear cut. For example, a patient with suicidal ideation can be offered an immediate appointment in the therapist's office to assess suicidal risk. While this may be a realistic option in the afternoon or early evening, a therapist may be understandably reluctant to offer an emergency appointment at 2:00 a.m., particularly in an isolated private practice office where no one else may be present. If the patient is directed to go to the local ED, a decision will have to be made about whether the patient can safely get to the ED, whether a family member or friend can be accessed to transport the patient, or whether an ambulance or police are required to drive the patient to the hospital. Each decision has implications, both for immediate management of suicide risk as well as for the treatment relationship. For example, if a patient is directed to go to the ED, the clinician must make a careful assessment and judgment about whether this can be done safely. For example, a patient having ideation about suicide by crashing his car would be a poor choice to drive himself to the ED. On the other hand, in some communities, it may be necessary to involve the police in order for alternative transport to be arranged. The experience of having the police or an ambulance arrive at a patient's home in the middle of the night, particularly if it is not with the patient's consent, may cause acute embarrassment and disrupt the collaboration so important to the therapeutic relationship. Thus, such decisions should be regarded as highly significant clinical decisions that require a careful weighing of risks and benefits, and these risks and benefits should be carefully documented.

Decisions regarding how to transport suicidal patients to an ED should be carefully made

It is stunning that despite the life and death nature of this type of decision making, there is virtually no empirical literature to guide clinicians, and clinicians rarely receive any kind of training regarding these issues.

Depending on the patient's location, the nearest ED can be reached within minutes or transport may take hours. Therapists should be aware of both the strengths and limitations of what EDs can do. While EDs are typically available around the clock, making them, along with crisis hotlines, one of the few 24-hour a day services available to patients at risk for suicide in the community, they are not available in every community, and the distance between the patient and the ED can often influence the operation of the emergency system. For example, in remote and frontier regions, access to a hospital might require air or helicopter transport, while in other areas multiple EDs may exist in the same community. Furthermore, it is important to be aware of the context in which many EDs operate. A recent Institute of Medicine Report, *The Future of Emergency Care,* (2006), found that many EDs in the U.S. are overcrowded, that emergency care is highly fragmented, and that critical specialists are often unavailable to provide emergency care (Giffin et al., 2006).

Mental health professionals such as psychiatrists and psychologists are sometimes unavailable in EDs. While it is possible that an ED affiliated with a teaching hospital will arrange for every suicidal patient to be seen by a psychiatric resident, in other EDs, particularly smaller, community hospitals in rural areas, there may be no mental health resources at all. If the therapist has privileges at the hospital, she will typically be asked to come in and see the patient, or will routinely be consulted about the disposition. If the therapist does not have privileges at the hospital, and, particularly if ED staff do not know them, the therapist might not be contacted at all. A meeting with ED staff prior to a crisis to review potential collaborations is recommended for all therapists working with suicidal patients. Particularly in EDs with limited mental health resources, the therapist's involvement can be of great assistance, as EDs need accurate information in order to provide a competent assessment of risk and need to have access to discharge resources. In a minority of hospitals, there will be a separate and designated psychiatric ED or service that will be in charge of the patient.

Under any circumstances, therapists can reasonably rely on several services being available in hospital EDs. First there will be a medical evaluation, which is of particular importance if the patient has engaged in some form of self-harming behavior. It is of vital importance, if the therapist has information regarding suicidal behavior that the patient has engaged in, that this be reported to the ED personnel, ideally to the physician. For example, if a patient has contacted the therapist and reported taking an overdose, it is important that the kind and amount of medication that the patient says they took be reported to the ED.

Any information the clinician may have on suicidal behavior should be reported to ED personnel

Second, suicidal patients will typically receive some kind of assessment of suicide risk in the ED, but this may not always be by a mental health professional. At times it may be done by the ED nurse or physician. Finally, every ED will arrange a disposition. However, such dispositions will often be heavily influenced by the available resources, such as inpatient psychiatric beds or outpatient mental health referrals.

In a study of response to suicidal patients in Californian emergency departments, Baraff, Janowicz, and Asarnow (2006) found that 23% of the EDs reported at times sending a patient home without receiving an evaluation from a mental health professional. Many did not have the capacity to admit to a

Clinical Vignette
Making Decisions About Emergency Transport

Jack telephoned his therapist at 11:00 p.m. and told her he was having suicidal thoughts. Jack was in treatment for posttraumatic stress disorder, and he had a history of one previous suicide attempt that had led to a psychiatric hospitalization. Jack and his therapist discussed coping strategies that he could utilize to get through the night, and his therapist offered him an appointment for the morning. However, after discussing with the patient and his wife Jack's ability to keep himself safe overnight, a conversation in which Jack expressed concern about his ability to not act on suicidal impulses, they agreed that he needed to be seen as soon as possible in the emergency room. They discussed the options of sending an ambulance versus having his wife drive him to the emergency department, which was approximately 20 minutes away from Jack's home. Jack felt confident he could keep himself safe during the drive, and his wife felt she could drive him safely. The therapist called both the on-call psychiatrist and the emergency department to inform them the patient would be arriving and to advise them regarding his current status. Jack arrived safely at the emergency department and was seen by the on-call psychiatrist.

Clinical Pearl
Information You Need to Know About Your Nearest Emergency Department

– What emergency department(s) is closest to your high risk patients?
– What transportation is available to take your patient to the emergency department?
– What kind of mental health coverage exists in the emergency department?
– Will the emergency department ask you to see your patient?
– Will the emergency department speak with you regarding disposition or providing follow-up appointments?

psychiatric bed in their own facility, and the average waiting time in the ED for transfer to a psychiatric bed in another facility was 7 hours. The majority of EDs reported that the availability of outpatient mental health resources to follow-up discharged patients was a problem, underscoring the importance of clinician's making EDs aware of their availability.

The recent findings that a brief ED intervention combined with sustained follow up reduced deaths by suicide (Fleischmann et al., 2008) underscores the importance for therapists of improving links with EDs.

4.2.5   Psychiatric Emergency Services

Another critical need for therapists is to have a clear understanding of the psychiatric emergency service system in their community. Communities vary greatly in the extent of psychiatric emergency resources available to them, so every therapist needs to have an understanding of this before commencing work with at risk, suicidal patients. Psychiatric emergency services may operate out of a hospital or from a community mental health center, and services provided may include ED coverage, emergent appointments in the mental health center, phone/hotline capacity, or mobile outreach teams. Psychiatric emergency services may also have access to additional services such as hospital-based crisis beds, alternative forms of crisis housing, or peer supports.

In most jurisdictions, ED psychiatrists are the individuals with the most expertise in how to get someone at risk hospitalized. This will typically include knowledge of how to access a hospital bed for an individual from a specialized population, such as children or the elderly. The best way, of course, for a clinician to be able to arrange a hospitalization is to have admitting privileges at a hospital himself or herself, or to have a close working relationship with a psychiatrist or other physician in order to arrange this. In many jurisdictions, the psychiatric emergency service may also be responsible for arranging involuntary hospitalizations.

4.2.6   Involuntary Hospitalization and the Use of the Police

The willingness and the capacity of patients to collaborate in keeping themselves safe is a critical variable that needs to be considered before using involuntary interventions. The risks and benefits must be carefully assessed and documented, as well as the patient's capacity and competence to enter into a collaborative plan to maintain his safety. For example, patients who are suicidal and intoxicated, or experiencing a psychotic episode as part of a schizophrenic or bipolar illness, or a delusional depression, may not have the capacity to collaboratively work to keep themselves safe. However, it must also be understood that the dispatching of police or ambulance against the patient's wishes is not always a benign intervention, regardless of the clinician's intentions. Such involuntary interventions may reduce imminent risk more dramatically than working with the patient collaboratively, but utilizing involuntary means is far from foolproof. The intervention may not be successful in bringing the patient to a secure setting (for example, the patient may flee the scene in advance of the police). At times the encounter is traumatic. If the patient does not agree to be transported, he or she may be restrained or put in handcuffs, with risk of potential injury to all concerned. In addition, the use of coercion may damage the therapeutic relationship, sometimes beyond repair. Unfortunately, despite the life and death nature of these decisions, there is very little research to help guide clinicians in this decision making. Amidst such uncertainty, knowledge of the patent's past behavior becomes particularly relevant.

> **The dispatching of police or ambulance against the patient's wishes is not always a benign intervention**

It is a significant challenge when the clinician believes a patient is at high, imminent risk of suicide but the patient is unwilling to collaborate in receiving emergency care. In such instances, it is essential to understand state law and the available psychiatric emergency resources. Such high stakes moments are not the time to begin learning how a system operates. Involuntary transport of patients at risk to EDs will often involve the utilization of police resources, and the ability of the police to intervene will typically vary from jurisdiction to jurisdiction. For example, some jurisdictions may require the police to personally observe evidence of dangerousness to self or others before intervening. The therapist's judgment, or statements made to the therapist, may not be sufficient in some circumstances to trigger involuntary transport.

4.2.7   Use of Mobile Outreach Services

Some jurisdictions will have a process as part of their psychiatric emergency response system that will allow a mobile outreach team to be utilized in such situations. Mobile outreach teams typically have the advantage of allowing for a suicide risk assessment to be done in the community, thereby avoiding the need for an involuntary transport for patients not found to be at high risk. It is often perplexing to patients as well as to police, that at times a patient may be brought involuntarily to a hospital ED, only to be discharged from the ED several hours later. However, there are numerous reasons that this can happen. EDs are responsible for making their own assessment of the patient once he or she enters the department. Risk can fluctuate over a period of hours, for example, as a blood alcohol level changes or as time passes from a stressful event. Also, the patient may have an incentive for concealing or minimizing upon interview in the ED the extent of their suicide risk in order to not be coerced to receive care. In addition, the ED may be influenced by issues such as lack of resources (e.g., a shortage of inpatient beds) that can lead to discharge from the ED, particularly when risk is ambiguous.

The use of mobile outreach teams can reduce the likelihood of such situations. Rather than bringing patients to the ED in order to receive an evaluation, that evaluation can take place in the community. Mobile outreach teams vary in their policies regarding going to private homes. Some insist on police accompaniment, so in some instances police involvement cannot be avoided, but the potential for being removed from one's home in handcuffs or restraints only to be released from the ED later can be minimized. In a national study, 39 states reported having implemented some form of mobile crisis services (Geller, Fisher, & McDermeit, 1995), although few had attempted any systematic evaluation of their impact. Several studies published since then have documented that mobile outreach teams may be effective as a diversion from psychiatric hospitalization.

Scott (2000) found that 55% of the emergencies handled by the mobile crisis team were managed without psychiatric hospitalization, compared with 28% of the emergencies handled by regular police intervention, a statistically significant difference. In a study by Hugo, Smout, and Bannister (2002), hospital-based emergency service contacts were found to be more than three times as likely to be admitted to a psychiatric inpatient unit when compared with those using a mobile community-based emergency service, regardless of their clinical characteristics. Similarly, a study by Dyches, Johnsen, & Oh (2002) of the impact of mobile crisis services on the use of mental health services found that, controlling for prior service use, mobile crisis intervention consumers with no prior mental health service use were 48% more likely to receive community-based mental health services within 90 days after the crisis event than a consumer receiving hospital-based interventions.

Mobile outreach services can reduce the need for police intervention and involuntary transport

It is very important to know whether your community has a mobile outreach team available in these circumstances. The availability of mobile outreach teams in communities in the US varies widely.

4.3   Safety Planning

Safety planning is an important component of managing suicidal patients on an outpatient basis. Assisting the patient in maintaining his or her own safety is important both during a crisis and during ongoing treatment. The central components of safety planning typically include involving family or significant others, means restriction, and assisting the patient in utilizing alternative coping behaviors. The central components of safety planning are widely accepted as important suicide prevention measures. Reducing access to lethal means, decreasing isolation, and increasing support by involving family or friends, and promoting alternative coping behaviors are recommended by most authorities (Bongar, 2002; Linehan, 1993). However, there has been some confusion in the field because of the superficial similarities between this type of safety planning and the use of "no-suicide contracts."

Safety plans, called crisis response plans by Rudd et al. (2001), rely on providing instructions or assistance for the patient to help promote what he or she can do when in crisis, rather than solely what he or she promises not to do. Intensive work is currently being undertaken to evaluate the effectiveness of safety planning as a separate intervention (Stanley & Brown, 2008).

Clinical Pearl
Denial of Suicidality: Cautions and Concerns

Clinicians often emphasize the patient's self-report regarding the presence or absence of suicidal thoughts. While this is clearly important information, it needs to be interpreted as part of a fuller assessment. Self-report can be influenced by both mood and context, and when we ask patients to tell us they won't attempt suicide over the next several days, we ask them to project into the future. The relationship between stated intent not to attempt suicide and the actual behavior, for example, for a patient who regularly abuses substances, can be tenuous indeed.

Busch et al. (2003) studied patients who died by suicide either in inpatient units or shortly after discharge. They found that a significant number denied/reported no suicidal ideation at their final clinical contact. The reported absence of suicidal ideation was therefore a poor predictor of short-term death by suicide, at least among patients in inpatient care. The precise reasons for this are not clear from the study. The influence of the context in which the assessment was taking place was one possibility. On an inpatient unit, reporting suicidal ideation can lead to continued hospitalization, at times involuntarily, and the potential for hospitalization can be a disincentive to honest disclosure. It is also possible that the patients were not suicidal at the time of the assessments, but that their suicidality recurred, again underscoring how suicide risk can fluctuate over hours, days, or weeks.

4.3.1   Involving Family and Friends

> "An essential predicate to my emotional health was to reduce my isola-
> tion. Ironically, that very sense of alienation was perpetuated by having
> to live in a private world of suicidal thoughts that I could not share with
> anyone – or so I thought." (Terry Wise, *Waking Up*, 2003, p. 3)

Social isolation is a significant risk factor for suicide, a finding that is among the most robust in suicide prevention. Therefore, interventions that reduce social isolation hold promise for suicide prevention. Yet, even those with supportive persons in their lives can feel isolated, particularly if they have been unwilling to share what they are going through. Shawn Shea (2002) puts it eloquently: "Death is sometimes chosen as the only alternative by people who feel deeply alone or shamed, yet are profoundly loved and respected" (p. 5). Encouraging self-disclosure to significant others of the depth of their pain and thoughts of suicide is therefore potentially important. Joiner (2005) has

Clinical Pearl
Components of Safety Planning:

- Provide emergency phone numbers
- Reduce access to lethal means
- Involve family and friends
- Promote alternate coping techniques

argued that failed belongingness and perceived burdensomeness are powerful risk factors for suicide. People need to feel connected to others and effective in those relationships; when they are disconnected and alone, and a burden to others rather than a help, they may wish to die. Efforts need to be made to deal with these issues directly in treatment, both in ongoing therapy and during a crisis. Potentially, a family session may help defuse a crisis and reduce risk. At minimum, family members need to be informed about how to access the clinician after hours or how to contact another 24-hour crisis service, such as a psychiatric emergency service or a suicide prevention hotline. This is particularly important given the research that those who make near lethal attempts are more likely to talk about suicide with families or friends than with health care professionals (Barnes et al., 2001).

In a crisis situation, families and significant others are often asked to provide a "suicide watch," that is to constantly observe the suicidal person to prevent them from making a suicide attempt. Except under extreme circumstances, this is neither necessary nor recommended. A person who requires constant observation to maintain safety should be hospitalized.

Educating families regarding suicide risk is extremely important. Naturally, we all prefer to believe our loved ones are not in danger, particularly in the absence of obvious signs of danger. So it is understandable for families to assume that when a relative is discharged from an inpatient psychiatric unit, he or she is no longer at risk, when in fact we know that this is a time of very high risk (Appleby et al., 1999). Similarly, families may misinterpret transient changes in mood as implying changes in longer term risk status. The fluctuating but enduring nature of suicide risk must be emphasized. Families should be coached to be available, alert, and open to communication. Families may need assistance with their own emotional responses to the stress of knowing that their loved one is at risk.

Education regarding warning signs should communicate what we know empirically as well as provide information that is patient specific. It is particularly important to communicate the need to take any discussion of suicide seriously. The willingness to ask directly about suicidal thoughts is critically important, along with instructions on how to respond if suicidal thoughts are present. If the patient and family feel that the presence of suicidal thoughts automatically means there must be an inpatient hospitalization, there may be a

Clinical Pearl
Family Involvement checklist

- Educate regarding suicide risk
- Discuss patient-specific warning signs
- Restrict lethal means
- Assure accessibility after hours
- Address perceived burdensomeness
- Enhance connectedness/reduce isolation

disincentive for honest communication. Openness regarding suicidal thoughts, while quite difficult, also holds the potential for reducing isolation.

An extremely important reason to involve the family or significant others is to gain their assistance in reducing access to lethal means. It is far better to have a friend or family member remove a weapon from a patient's home, for example, rather than asking the patient to get a firearm out of the house, which would require him to handle the very weapon he is contemplating using to kill himself.

4.3.2   Means Restriction

The restriction of lethal means is one of the most frequently emphasized and best validated suicide prevention strategies, and it is particularly important during times of acute risk. Means restrictions strategies can be population based or individualized clinical interventions. Barriers on bridges, carbon monoxide technologies, coal gasification and paracetamol restrictions have shown impressive impacts on suicide mortality (Beautrais, 2007). Goal 5 of the National Strategy for Suicide Prevention is to Promote Efforts to Reduce Access to Lethal Means and Methods to Self-Harm (U.S. Department of Health and Human Services, 2001); this goal was included because of the strong evidence supporting such measures.

The reason that such strategies can be effective is that most people are ambivalent about dying by suicide and so many do not substitute alternative lethal methods. While the literature on the use of means restriction as a public health measure is robust, the literature on the clinical use of means restrictions strategies is not as well researched. However, based on the public health literature, clinical means restriction strategies should be considered to be based on a solid empirical foundation. A frequently used means restriction strategy, for example, is for prescribers of medication to manage the amount of medication available to prevent its use in a potentially lethal overdose. Another particularly important area of inquiry is the availability of firearms. It is important to ask about firearms availability, even if the patient has not indicated that it is a method of suicide he is thinking about. Firearms are highly lethal, and unlike some other means of suicide, the act cannot be aborted once it has begun. For example, a person may begin to ingest pills in a suicide attempt, but as they are in the process of overdosing decide that they do want to live. It is not uncommon on crisis lines to speak to people who have begun an overdose and stopped. Unfortunately, such "second thoughts" are not possible when firearms are used.

It is important to ask about firearms availability, even if a patient has not indicated anything about this method

Additionally, instructing individuals or family members to reduce or eliminate access to lethal means is also a frequent recommendation, despite the challenges inherent in this task. However, there is some evidence supporting this clinical approach. For example, Kruesi et al. (1999) developed an approach for use in EDs, although the model could be easily adapted to other settings, including outpatient psychotherapy. They utilized a three-step method to educate parents of youth at high risk for suicide who received mental health assessments in EDs. The intervention could be accomplished in five minutes in busy emergency rooms. The three steps included informing parents that their adolescent was at risk for suicide and why the clinician thought so, tell-

A three-step approach was found effective in reducing access to firearms among adolescents

ing the parents they can reduce the risk of suicide by getting firearms out of the house, and educating parents about different ways to dispose of or limit access to a firearm. Follow-up telephone interviews of parents indicated that exposure to the intervention resulted in a statistically significant increase in the self-reported restriction of means in the home.

Additionally, one cannot presume that patients will automatically adhere to recommendations to remove lethal means. This is where the family may play a critical role. It is always preferable to have a family member or friend be the person who actually removes firearms or other lethal means. The clinician wants to avoid inadvertently creating a high risk moment by having a suicidal person with a firearm in his hand. However, even family members may not adhere to recommendations to remove firearms. In a study by Brent, Baugher, Birmather, Kolko, and Bridge (2000), only 27% of parents of depressed adolescents were found to have removed firearms after having received a clinical recommendation to do so to reduce suicide risk. For this reason a phone follow-up is strongly recommended. It is also important that clinicians do not allow their own personal feelings about guns to color their clinical interventions. Many Americans greatly value gun ownership and adherence to clinical recommendations is likely to be poor if these views are not respected.

A higher risk of suicide is associated with handguns compared to long guns, with unlocked more than locked guns, and with loaded more than unloaded guns (Brent, 2001). Simon (2007), in a review of the principles of gun safety management, recommended that clinicians inquire about guns at home or located outside the home (e.g., car, office, etc.) when working with suicidal patients. They should also ask if their patient intends to purchase or obtain a firearm. When firearms need to be removed, it is recommended that the patient designate a willing, responsible person to remove and secure guns and ammunition to a location outside the home that is unknown to the patient, and that the clinician confirm with the designated person that the firearms and ammunition have been removed. Simon further recommend that patients in emergency departments and inpatient units not be discharged until this is accomplished (Simon, 2007).

4.3.3   Safety Planning Versus No-Suicide Contracts

"Suicide is not beholden to an evening's promises, nor does it always hearken to plans drawn up in lucid moments and banked in good intentions." (Jamison, 1999)

One of the most controversial areas in the treatment of suicidal persons is the use of "no-suicide contracts." No-suicide contracts are also sometimes referred to as "no-harm contracts," "safety contracts," or "suicide prevention contracts." Despite the lack of evidence to support their efficacy as a suicide prevention technique, their use is reported to be widespread. According to the Institute of Medicine report, "Suicide prevention contracts are widely used in all mental health settings as risk management tools, but they remain poorly evidenced" (Goldsmith et al., 2002, p. 291). In her 2007 review, Lewis describes suicide contracts as "standard practice in the treatment of suicidal ideation" (p. 50). In their basic form, no-suicide contracts are simply promises not to kill oneself.

No-suicide contracts can be verbal or written. When written, they typically include a statement in which the patient agrees not to attempt suicide. Written contracts are typically signed by both the patient and therapist. They may include an alternative that the patient agrees to engage in when feeling suicidal, such as calling their therapist or a suicide prevention hotline (Lewis, 2007).

Despite the lack of evidence supporting their use, no-suicide contracts must serve functions for clinicians or they wouldn't be used so widely and so often. The IOM further reports, "...there is a general perception that they are helpful" (Goldsmith et al., 2002, p. 291). To understand this, we should examine the context in which these contracts are typically used. Most frequently, these are used when there are circumstances leading to concerns about increased risk, and there is a need to decide upon an intervention to respond to this increased risk.

No-suicide contracts provide a straight forward technique for making a complex, clinical judgment, a judgment often fraught with anxiety and uncertainty. If the suicidal person is willing to "contract for safety," she or he is likely to be treated as an outpatient. If she or he is not willing, then hospitalization is the answer. Frequently, the consequence of refusal to agree to a no-suicide contract may be involuntary hospitalization (Lewis, 2007). There may be motivation to go along with such contracts in order to avoid unwanted outcomes. Obtaining a no-suicide contract may therefore reduce a clinician's anxiety, but it also may play an inordinately influential role in clinical decision making. This is of particular concern given Farrow, Simpson, and Warren's (2002) finding that clients tended to experience the contracts as a barrier to talking about their suicidal thoughts. Thus, rather than assisting clients to talk openly about their thoughts, allowing clinicians to make a more informed estimate of suicide risk, and collaboratively make a decision about the need for hospitalization, no suicide contracts may inadvertently encourage concealment by the client and less informed and thorough risk assessment by the clinician. This may be particularly problematic if contracts are a substitute for more empirically justifiable interventions, such as means restriction or involving the family. No-suicide contracts are typically used as a justification for outpatient treatment, or for readiness for discharge from inpatient units or EDs.

Agreement to no-suicide contracts are often heavily influenced by the potential consequences of refusal

No-suicide contracts are not part of the formal written tradition of suicide assessment. More often their use is perpetuated by word of mouth, and clinician's have not received formal training in their use. Their popularity may well reflect the absence of training in suicide risk assessment and treatment experienced by many of the mental health professions (Goldsmith et al., 2002)

Refusal to sign such a contract does not mean a patient is at imminent risk, nor does agreement mean that risk is lessened (Goldsmith et al., 2002). Patients' motivations for signing or refusing to sign a contract are complex, and one risk of using no-suicide contracts is that they may provide a false sense of security to the clinician and cause lessened diligence about the possibility of suicide (Simon, 1999).

No-suicide contracts should never be used in place of appropriate suicide risk assessment and treatment

Part of the confusion around no-suicide contracts involves the recognition that these techniques combine suicide prevention techniques that are misguided with those that are valuable. For example, a competent assessment must explore whether the patient intends to die by suicide. Attempting to gain a commitment to work on staying alive is a component of empirically supported treatments such as DBT. When no-suicide contracts include elements of a safety plan, such as provision of a phone number to call when feeling suicidal and removal of potentially lethal means such as firearms from the patient's environment or the involvement of family or significant others to form a supportive network around the patient, they may be of real value.

The dilemma is in relying solely on the patient's promise that he or she will not attempt to kill him-/herself rather than implementing a comprehensive safety plan. Promises to not attempt suicide, even when given in good faith, assume the patient can accurately anticipate the recurrence and intensity of their suicidal urges. Particularly for those with substance abuse problems or psychotic symptoms, this can be extremely difficult.

Several studies have found that many of those who made suicide attempts or died by suicide had a no-suicide contract in place

According to the Office of the Ombudsman for Mental Health and Mental Retardation, State of Minnesota (2002), no-suicide contracts were in place for almost every suicide that occurred in an inpatient, acute care facility. Other studies have also found that a significant number of those who made suicide attempts or died by suicide had such contracts in place at the time of their suicidal act (APA, 2003).

4.4   Treatment Techniques

Treatment Targets

Most treatments for suicidal persons advocate some form of targeting for pursuing work in therapy. The therapist must have a clear idea of how to proceed and what must be prioritized. Shneidman (1996) believes that the implications of the ten commonalities of suicide for psychotherapy are to "reduce the pain: remove the blinders, lighten the pressure" (p. 139). As suicide is an effort to escape from unendurable pain, reducing the pain is a crucial priority. Any lessening of the pain may assist in making the intolerable tolerable. Both promoting change and enhancing acceptance can be viable means for doing this. Problem solving pressing and painful problems may successfully reduce the pressure and thus the press towards suicide. Alternatively, pain can at times be reduced through acceptance, by no longer struggling to resist a reality that cannot be changed.

In DBT, treatment targets are set according to a defined hierarchy. This hierarchy is determined not by how many weeks or months of treatment have taken place, but instead by the behaviors in which the patient is engaging. Suicidal behavior is always the first priority, and nothing else can be addressed in individual therapy sessions until the suicidal behavior is thoroughly analyzed. If no suicidal behavior has taken place, the second priority is therapy interfering behavior (Linehan, 1993). This is any behavior, by either patient or therapist, that threatens the therapeutic relationship. The notion here is that therapy is frequently terminated by either the patient or the therapist when one of them unilaterally becomes frustrated and ends the treatment. Therefore, any interactions that threaten the treatment must be thoroughly examined. If neither suicidal behavior or therapy interfering behavior are present, the next target is quality of life interfering behaviors, behaviors that while not life threatening, make a life worth living impossible, for example substance abuse.

4.4.1   Skills Training

Skills training as a therapeutic means for reducing the risk of suicidal behavior has been most extensively developed in DBT. In DBT, skills training is a central focus, with patients expected to participate in a weekly skills training group throughout a year of treatment. The goal is to help patients actively problem solve life's challenges using an array of skills. There is a focus in DBT on assisting the patient in acquiring skills, strengthening skills, and in generalizing skills to differing situations and contexts (Linehan, 1993). Acquiring new skills is the focus of the skills training group using didactic instruction, role plays, and other methods. While individual therapy can also be a setting for such instruction, for people in suicidal crisis it may be difficult to systematically attend in individual therapy to such skills training. The goal in individual therapy is to get the patient to utilize the skills he or she is learning in the group.

The DBT skills training modules (mindfulness, interpersonal effectiveness, emotional regulation, and distress tolerance) are presented sequentially, and the teaching of the skills is the most important task during the conduct of the group. Thus, a patient who began to speak about suicide during the group would not become the focus of attention. The group therapist would guide the group back to the teaching of skills through a comment such as "I understand that you're feeling suicidal right now, but that underscores for me the importance of your learning these skills and being able to use them to have a life worth living."

> DBT skills include modules on mindfulness, interpersonal effectiveness, emotional regulation, and distress tolerance

Of the four types of skills taught in DBT, mindfulness is likely the least familiar to clinicians. Influenced by Eastern philosophy, mindfulness focuses on cultivating an awareness of the present moment. Mindfulness skills also build on the central insight that while we can control what we do, we have very limited control over what we think and feel. We don't decide what thought we will have, nor do we decide what emotion we will experience. Yet we tend to identify ourselves with our thoughts and emotions, and we overestimate the extent to which our thoughts and feelings are under conscious control. We can, however, learn to control what we pay attention to. For millennia, techniques such as meditation and yoga have been used to enhance this attentional control. In addition to Linehan's work, using mindfulness with chronically suicidal persons who met diagnostic criteria for borderline personality disorder, mindfulness has also now been utilized in the treatment of depression (Teasdale et al., 2000). Examples of the mindfulness skills taught in DBT include "observing," a process that involves the skill of observing the inner flow of experience. Another example is describing experience rather than judging it. For example, "my boss treated me terribly" would be a judgment. In contrast, "my boss shouted at me" would be a description.

Mindfulness stands in direct opposition to the desire to die by suicide

The importance of mindfulness as a fundamental skill in DBT is underscored by returning to review mindfulness skills after each of the other skills training modules is completed. In many ways, cultivation of mindfulness stands in direct opposition to the desire to die by suicide. Shneidman described the common goal in suicide to be the cessation of consciousness and the ending of awareness; in contrast, mindfulness aims to enhance conscious awareness. While it is not yet known what role mindfulness skills play in DBTs effectiveness, its potential seems clear.

Crisis survival skills help the suicidal person get through the crisis without resorting to self-destructive behavior

Distress tolerance includes two components: One component focuses on crisis survival skills while the other attempts to teach deeper forms of acceptance. Crisis survival skills involve techniques designed to help the suicidal person get through the crisis without resorting to self-destructive behavior. They are not designed to solve the problems that are leading a person to be suicidal in the first place, rather they are intended to help the person stay alive long enough to have a chance to solve those problems. Various forms of distraction would be examples of crisis survival strategies. For instance, holding an ice cube in the hand and focusing on the intense sensation of cold can be a potential distractor from suicidal urges. The other component of distress tolerance skills involves accessing deeper levels of acceptance; Linehan (1993) calls this practice "radical acceptance."

Emotional regulation, distress tolerance, and self-monitoring skills should be core interventions in working with suicidal patients

Emotional regulation skills blend teaching about the nature of emotions based on current scientific research, with the learning of skills that can help change emotional experiences through behavior change. For example, the skill of "opposite action" involves exposure principles, such as approaching what you fear, and being open and not hiding when experiencing shame.

Interpersonal effectiveness skills are perhaps the most familiar for clinicians, incorporating elements of treatments such as assertiveness training while maintaining an emphasis on "doing what's effective."

Rudd at al. (2001) also emphasize the importance of skill building in their time-limited cognitive behavioral therapy as well, identifying emotional regulation, distress tolerance and self-monitoring to be core interventions that should be standard in working with suicidal patients regardless of the specifics of the clinical presentation.

4.4.2   Self Monitoring/Homework Assignments

The importance of homework assignments, like that of telephone interventions, rests on an understanding that the goal of therapy is to enhance the patient's ability to cope with suicidal thoughts and urges in their day-to-day life outside of the therapy session.

Both DBT and CBT incorporate the use of homework assignments. In DBT, the skills training group exposes patients systematically to the skills of mindfulness, interpersonal effectiveness, emotional regulation, and distress tolerance, and assigns homework to practice the skills that have been taught each week. The individual therapist has the task of encouraging and persuading the patient to use these skills in their daily life. In order to be able to utilize these skills in a suicidal crisis it is essential that patients have practiced them when they are not emotionally overwhelmed. In DBT, skills training com-

Clinical Vignette

Chain Analysis of Suicidal Behavior

Janet was a 27-year-old female who cut her wrists following an upsetting encounter in the department store in which she worked. At her next therapy session after she had cut her wrists, she worked together with her therapist to identify the chain of events, both external and internal, that had led to her self-destructive act. They then reviewed skills she could have utilized as alternatives at each step.

Chain Analysis	Solution Analysis
Argument with customer in store	Interpersonal effectiveness skills
Thinks, "I can't stand this anymore"	Distress tolerance/radical acceptance
Quits job and leaves store	Interpersonal effectiveness skills
Thinks, "I've failed again' and feels ashamed	Describing rather than judging, mindfulness
Goes to car and cuts self with razor	Distraction/crisis survival skills

mences at the very start of treatment. In CBT, there is an emphasis first on cognitive modification, and then on skills development, with homework assignments being utilized for both.

Both Rudd et al. (2001) and Linehan (1993) emphasize the importance of self-monitoring. Rudd et al. recommend the use of a treatment log in which the patient makes entries at the end of each session. In DBT, the patient fills out a diary card on a daily basis. The diary cards include ratings of the intensity of suicidal ideation/urges, as well as whether suicidal behavior occurs. The use of skills being taught in the skills training group is also recorded. Review of the diary cards is the first task in individual therapy each week. If suicidal behavior has taken place, it becomes the immediate focus of the session. In DBT, patients are required, when they have engaged in suicidal behavior, to fill out a detailed, behavioral chain analysis of the episode examining vulnerability factors, precipitating events, and consequences of the suicidal behavior. The patient therefore develops an increasing awareness of what leads to and reinforces her suicidal behavior, rather than experiencing the suicidal behavior as coming "out of the blue" in a sudden rush of emotion. At each step of the chain that leads to the suicidal behavior, specific action steps are identified that can be used in the future as alternative more skillful behaviors that can be utilized. This is referred to as a solution analysis.

4.4.3 Cognitive Interventions

Most cognitive behavioral therapies include a similar range of interventions, although they may vary in the emphasis given to specific interventions. All cognitive behavioral treatments contain cognitive interventions, but in some approaches, such as Rudd et al. (2001) and Brown et al. (2006), these interventions are more central. The private meaning assigned by the suicidal individual to his or her experience and the core beliefs about self, other, and the world, are each imbued with some level of hopelessness. Regardless of the specific personal meaning, Rudd et al. (2001) recommend a core set of techniques to use to modify the suicidal belief system. They captured this approach in the acronym ICARE:

Identify	identifying the automatic thoughts and core beliefs
Connect	connect these thoughts to cognitive distortions
Assess	assess or evaluate the evidence for these beliefs
Restructure	constructing a more realistic belief
Execute	act as though the new belief is true, performing a behavioral experiment to disconfirm the original dysfunctional belief

Although DBT focuses on the role of behavior and emotion, rather than on cognitions, it also includes cognitive modification procedures, although they are used more informally and less systematically than in Rudd's model. Clarifying current contingencies is an example of a cognitive technique used in DBT. Recognizing the negative consequences of suicide attempts would be another example of this technique. Suicide attempts typically serve a function in the short run (e.g., they help the patient escape pain), but these attempts cause more problems in the long run and are thus counterproductive. Helping patients understand this is an example of clarifying current contingencies.

4.4.4   Exposure Treatment

Linehan has also identified the role of exposure-based techniques in treating suicidal behavior (Linehan, 1993). For patients with borderline personality dis-

Clinical Vignette
Exposure Techniques in Practice

Therapist:	It sounds like it was a very difficult weekend.
Patient:	It was.
Therapist:	You were very upset your son didn't call.
Patient:	I'm feeling suicidal.
Therapist:	You're feeling suicidal right now?
Patient:	Yes.
Therapist:	When did you start to think about suicide?
Patient:	Just a minute ago.
Therapist:	What was happening just before you started thinking about suicide?
Patient:	When you mentioned my son.
Therapist:	When I mentioned you were very upset that your son didn't call, you immediately began to think about suicide?
Patient:	Yes.
Therapist:	What I would like to do now is to repeat what I had said, and what I would like you to do is to try to focus on observing the feelings that you have in response and then describe them to me. This is part of helping you cope with intense feelings without becoming suicidal. Is that OK?
Patient:	I'll try.
Therapist:	Here goes. You were very upset when your son didn't call over the weekend.
Patient:	Yes.
Therapist:	What did you notice that you felt when I said that?
Patient:	I felt very angry.

order, almost any intense emotional experience may trigger suicidal behavior in an effort to escape the emotional intensity. More broadly, suicidal behavior can be conceptualized as escape or avoidance behavior, an effort to block or get away from experiences that seem intolerable. For chronically suicidal patients, this can be almost an automatic response. Suicidal ideation itself can have this function. The thought of suicide reduces, at least momentarily, the experience of painful emotions, and suicidal thinking is thus reinforced and more likely to be repeated. To change this automatic response requires the painful emotion to be experienced while blocking the escape that the thought of suicide provides. This can be worked on repeatedly during the therapy session. An example is provided in the Clinical Vignette on Exposure techniques in practice.

4.4.5   Reducing Perceived Burdensomeness

Perceived burdensomeness is an important risk factor for suicide (Joiner, 2005). According to Joiner it is one of the most important reasons people want to kill themselves. When patients are at increased risk and perceive they are a burden to others, particularly to loved ones, they may believe that death by suicide will remove that burden from loved ones. While it is true that mental illness can have an impact on friends and family, and that chronic mental illness in particular may impose some burdens, it is rare that this burden will be greater than the lifelong burden carried by loved ones who have experienced a death by suicide. Addressing perceived burdensomeness is complicated by the fact that suicidal behavior itself creates burden for caretakers. In an important study of the impact of current suicidal ideation and past suicide attempts by bipolar patients on caregiver burden, caregivers for suicidal patients with suicidal histories had greater burden and poorer health than caregivers for bipolar patients without such histories (Chessick, Perlick, Miklowitz, Kaczynski, Allen, Morris, & Marangel, 2007). Suicide attempts in particular seemed to have a strong impact. The suicide attempt of a spouse or family member is an experience that can have enduring effects for years to come. Such complexities need to be kept in mind when dealing with these issues clinically. The patient's perception that he or she is a burden may be at least partially true, so simple reassurance that the patient is not a burden may be insufficient and lack credibility. At the same time, it may be the pain of almost losing a loved one to suicide and living with that fear over time that creates such burden. However, the response of survivor's when such fears come to pass is more likely to be devastation than relief. So the key therapeutic task may be to help the patient recognize that while there may be some burden that is imposed on family by their illness, the magnitude of that burden pales in comparison to the burdens experienced by loved ones following a death by suicide.

A key therapeutic task is to help the patient recognize the devastation experienced by loved ones following a death by suicide

An excellent example of the use in psychotherapy of helping a suicidal person grasp the depth of the devastation their suicide would create comes from Terry Wise's account (2003) of her near fatal suicide attempt, and her psychotherapy both before and after the attempt. Terry recounts how her therapist systematically and relentlessly led her through the impact her suicide would have on all those she loved. This was not easy work. "I hated having to say the words that brought the horrid consequences to life" (Wise, 2003). The

Clinical Pearl
Strategies For Addressing Perceived Burdensomeness

Sustained psychotherapeutic exploration

Family session

Normalization with physical illness

Sharing of the survivor literature

"This was the first time I felt my rationalization no one would be seriously affected by my suicide being jeopardized." (Terry Wise)

goal is not to make the suicidal person feel guilty, or to persuade them that they ought to live in order to spare other's feelings, but rather to help them cast a clear, realistic eye on the actual consequences of their suicide and to break down the tunnel vision and cognitive constriction characteristic of the suicidal mind. Again, from Wise's account, "…the intensity was necessary in order to shake the roots of my long standing beliefs. This was the first time I felt my rationalization no one would be seriously affected by my suicide being jeopardized (2003, p.137).

Another technique is to normalize the experience of burden by equating it to physical illness. Diabetes and heart disease pose burdens on families as well but typically far less than the patient's death would impose. Finally, the survivor literature can be utilized to help the suicidal patient achieve a more balanced understanding of what their death by suicide would mean to those they love. Books such as *My Son, My Son* by Iris Bolton (1984) clearly underscore the depth of pain caused by suicide.

4.4.6   Failed Belongingness

Joiner (2005) proposes, based on his review of the scientific literature, that the two major reasons people want to kill themselves are that they perceive themselves as a burden to others and that they feel that they do not belong. The notion that social integration protects against suicide, while social isolation intensifies risk, is one of the oldest findings in suicidology (Durkheim, 1897) . It is also noteworthy that social withdrawal is frequently experienced in depression. While feeling connected to family, friends, and community is protective against suicide, this protection is not absolute, as desire for suicide can also be intensified by feeling like a burden to those one loves. Nevertheless, promoting social connection and a sense of belonging should be considered an important goal of psychotherapy.

A therapeutic relationship is no replacement for a sense of connecting and belonging with family, friends, and community

For persons at risk in therapy, the connection to the therapist is extremely important for suicide prevention, and it underscores the importance of being able to rapidly establish a collaborative relationship. However, as important as the relationship with the therapist is, it is not a replacement for an enduring connection and sense of belonging with family, friends, and community. A potentially useful strategy to promote connection and belongingness is to assess what the client's most important values in life have been and provide assistance in connecting or re-connecting with organizations that may share those values (e.g., churches, social causes). This can lead not only to a greater sense of belonging, but also to a greater sense of effectiveness. For many people at risk for suicide, previous meaningful relationships may have faded. Reconnecting with family and friends who were once valued relationships can be a very important intervention.

4.4.7   Bibliotherapy

There are a number of ways in which bibliotherapy can be of benefit. Both CBT and DBT (Ellis & Newman, 1996; Linehan, 1993) provide a manual to aid patients with utilizing the skills and techniques provided in therapy sessions. Such materials help support both approaches and emphasis on homework assignments promote practice of coping skills outside of sessions. Such aids serve an important bridging function, so that patients do not have to rely solely on their memory of instructions or advice given in psychotherapy sessions. In addition, bibliotherapy focused on the diagnostic conditions that may be precipitating a suicidal crisis, such as psychoeducational books on depression, bipolar disorder, or substance abuse, can also be of value.

Another potential use of bibliotherapy relates to the issue of perceived burdensomeness as a risk factor, as emphasized by Joiner (2005). Frequently patients, particularly those who have been struggling with a mental illness over a period of time, will experience themselves as being a burden to their family or loved ones. With the cognitive constriction typical of suicidal persons, they are frequently unaware of the devastating burden that their suicide would impose on all those who care about them, or else rationalize that the pain caused by their mental illness or other problems outweighs the pain that would be caused by their suicide. This is rarely true. To attempt to change this misperception, it can be helpful to recommend readings from the survivor literature (see Table 11). This poignant literature provides accounts of deaths by suicide from the perspective of bereaved family members, describing the anguish that they have experienced. Being familiar with this literature, which presents the experience of loss from the perspective of parent, sibling, spouse etc, can allow the clinician to expose the person considering suicide to a far more realistic view of

Table 11
Family Survivor Literature:

- *My Son...My Son: A Guide to Healing After Death, Loss, or Suicide* (1984)
  Iris Bolton with C. Mitchell (parent survivor)
- *No Time To Say Goodbye: Surviving the Suicide of a Loved One* (1999)
  Carla Fine (spouse survivor)
- *Do They Have Bad Days in Heaven? Surviving the Suicide Loss of a Sibling* (2001)
  Michelle Linn-Gust (sibling survivor)
- *Touched by Suicide: Hope and Healing after Suicide* (2006)
  Mike Meyers and Carla Fine (spouse survivor)
- *After a Suicide: A Workbook for Grieving Kids* (2001)
  The Dougy Center (child survivor)

the likely impact on their loved ones if they go through with the lethal act. Presentation of this material needs to be handled sensitively. The intent is not simply to try to make the patient feel guilty for considering suicide, but rather to give them a clearer perspective on what their death would actually mean. While these books are typically written to help other survivors cope, and are highly recommended for use by therapists for that purpose, they can be of help to the suicidal person themselves.

Books that recount the experience of going through a suicidal crisis and emerging ultimately with a life worth living can also be valuable (see Table 12). Such books, by people who know what it is like to face this dark night of the soul, promote hope. *Waking Up*, by Terry Wise, can be of particular value for psychotherapy patients as her relationship with her therapist is a central part of the book. For families dealing with a suicidal adolescent, the book *Will's Choice* presents the experience of an adolescent who makes a near lethal suicide attempt, from the point of view of his mother (Griffith, 2005).

Table 12
Survivors of Suicidal Crises

- *Night Falls Fast* (1999)
  Kay Redfield Jamison
- *Waking Up* (2004)
  Terry Wise
- *Eight Stories Up* (2008)
  De Quincy Lezine
- *Darkness Visible* (1990)
  William Styron
- *Will's Choice* (2005)
  Gail Griffith
- *Children of Jonah* (2001)
  James Clemons (Ed.)

4.4.8   Outreach and Follow-up

When therapy comes to a planned conclusion, it is useful to schedule one or two additional sessions several months after therapy has ended. These return visits may function as booster sessions where the patient's coping can be reviewed, recurrence of suicidality can be assessed for, and the use of skillful alternatives to suicidal behavior can be reinforced.

An excellent brief intervention that can be used following both planned and premature terminations from treatment is the use of brief, caring letters. This approach was first studied by Jerome Motto (Motto & Bostrum, 2001). Patients hospitalized for suicide risk were contacted 30 days after discharge. Those patients who had either refused or discontinued therapy were random- ized to either an experimental or control condition. The intervention was a brief letter sent to them by a researcher who had interviewed them while they were hospitalized. The note simply said:

> Dear _____ ,
> It has been a while since you were here at the hospital and we hope things are going well for you. If you wish to drop us a note we would be glad to hear from you.

A self-addressed, un-stamped envelope was enclosed, and if the person wrote back, their letter was answered. After two years, the experimental group that had received the letters had significantly fewer suicides than the control, no-contact group. While at the five-year follow-up this effect was no longer statistically significant, the study provides strong support for the value of routinely incorporating such letters into treatment of high-risk suicidal patients, particularly those that drop out of treatment. The results of the Fleischmann et al. (2008) ED follow-up study also provide support that episodic but sustained contact may have great value.

A similar study was conducted by Carter et al. (2005). Patients who presented to an emergency department with deliberate self-poisoning (intentional overdoses) received a non-demanding postcard (enclosed in an envelope) at set intervals, between 30 days and twelve months after the suicide attempt. While there were not any differences in the proportion of patients in the two groups who made repeat attempts, the number of repeat attempts was reduced by 50% in the experimental group. There was also a significant decrease in the number of hospital days used associated with the decrease in the number of attempts.

Combined, the results of the Motto and Bostrun (2001) and the Carter et al. (2005) studies provide persuasive evidence that high-risk patients who drop out of treatment, and are unable to be re-engaged by telephone outreach, should receive non-demanding letters periodically. Given the low-risk, low-cost nature of the intervention, combined with the large potential benefit, such letters should become a standard part of practice with suicidal patients.

4.4.9   Postvention

4.4.9.1   Responding to the Aftermath of Suicide Attempts
"Finding empathy for a suicide attempt is as unlikely as killing your parents and receiving sympathy for being an orphan," wrote Terry Wise (2003, p. 131)

In addition to the need for crisis intervention in the immediate aftermath of a suicide attempt, which includes the need for medical evaluation and a suicide risk assessment to determine whether psychiatric hospitalization is necessary, suicide attempts have consequences and implications that must be thoroughly explored in ongoing psychotherapy.

These consequences range from the impact of the suicide attempt on the therapy relationship, the impact on family and friends, potential impact on job status and financial status, as well as the effect on the individual's sense of self-efficacy and self-esteem. The suicide attempt also has implications that must be explored in order to prevent future suicide attempts. There is a need to thoroughly analyze all the steps leading to the suicide attempt in order to determine how alternative solutions can be promoted in the future. Each possible turning point on the road to the suicide attempt must be identified. Linehan (1993), as previously described, utilizes a behavioral chain analysis combined with a solution analysis in order to accomplish this.

In *Waking Up*, Terry Wise, provides a compelling example of a therapist and a client grappling with the aftermath of a suicide attempt. Understanding the impact on family and friends can also be crucial. Suicide attempts are powerful interpersonal events that set off reverberations that must be understood and coped with. If not addressed in therapy, suicide attempts can lead either to increased isolation, if no one is able to talk about what has happened, or increased conflict, if the suicide attempt is experienced by others as either an expression of anger towards them or a sign that the suicidal individual doesn't care about the family.

Suicide attempts are powerful interpersonal events that must be understood and coped with

A suicide attempt should also lead to a re-evaluation of the treatment plan. While the fact that a suicide attempt takes place doesn't always mean that the treatment plan needs to be changed, particularly if suicide risk is already clearly and comprehensively being addressed in the treatment plan, a suicide attempt should always lead to a review so that the clinician can see if he or she can identify anything being missed.

A suicide attempt should always lead to a review of the treatment plan

4.4.9.2   Responding to Deaths By Suicide

Undoubtedly, losing a patient to suicide is one of the most difficult and traumatic events that therapists can experience in their professional lives. Like all survivors of suicide, the therapist is likely to experience both powerful and conflicting emotions. Also, like all survivors of suicide, therapists are likely to ask themselves many questions about their own actions prior to the death.

However, the therapist's efforts to work through his or her own grief and doubt may be complicated by processes of administrative review and concerns about legal liability For years systematic review of deaths by suicide in mental health treatment have been relatively rare, which is likely a reflection of the more generalized difficulty in talking about suicide that afflicts our entire society. More recently, however, organizations such as the Joint Commission and the Veterans Healthcare Administration have mandated root cause analyses of deaths by suicide. The heart of a root cause analysis is to look for systems issues that can be learned from and corrected, rather than to identify personal fault or blame. For therapists working outside of organized healthcare delivery system, a similar "root cause analysis" should be undertaken within the context of a group practice or supervision group. State law should be consulted to determine whether in the clinician's locality this is subject to legal discovery. The death of a patient by suicide does not necessarily mean that a therapist has done something wrong, anymore than a death during surgery means that a surgeon made a mistake during the surgery. However, we owe it to all those we treat, as well as their families, to routinely review all deaths by suicide that occur while in treatment, to maximize what we can learn and how we can improve our practice in order to better help others.

Deaths by suicide should be reviewed to maximize what we can learn and to improve practice

A particularly important question is how to respond to the family of the person who has died by suicide. If the therapist has already involved them in the treatment, they will not be strangers, but if not, this could be the therapist's first contact. Bennett et al. (2006) emphasize that a therapist's actions should be governed by whether the therapist can be of benefit to the family.

"When permitted by state law, you may discuss some of the general therapeutic issues with the patient's family, share your condolences, and try to give the family a sense of closure. Not only is this the humane thing to do, it also reduces your risk of being sued if you are open, caring, and forthright with the family" (Bennett et al, 2006. p. 170) .

As part of these discussions with the family, providing resources to assist the family in coping with the immensity of their loss may be appropriate. In some communities, survivors of suicide groups exist in which the surviving family members can be supported by others who understand the enormity of the pain they are experiencing. Information on survivor of suicide groups is available from national suicide prevention groups such as the American Association of Suicidology (www.suicidology.org), the American Foundation for Suicide Prevention (www.afsp.org), or the Suicide Prevention Action Network (www.spanusa.org), among others.

Referring family members or close friends to a group for survivors of suicide should be considered

Referral for therapy may also be appropriate. Clinicians who survive the loss of a client should refer the surviving family members to colleagues (Dunne, 1992).

4.5   Mechanisms of Action

The research evidence in the suicide prevention literature is too sparse to specify with certainty the mechanisms of action for programs with some evidence of effectiveness. Many of the approaches with some evidence of success have utilized multiple component interventions. For example, it is unknown if the effectiveness of the Air Force Suicide Prevention Program, which reduced suicide by 33%, was due to the promotion of a culture of shared responsibility for intervening with those at risk for suicide, which may have reduced social isolation and enhanced belongingness, to the encouragement of help seeking, to the universal accessibility of health care services, or to some combination of these factors (Knox, Litts, Talcott, Feig, & Caine, 2003). The program's success in also reducing episodes of serious domestic violence, accidental deaths, and homicides suggests that the program had an impact on shared risk and protective factors across these different, severe problems. Similarly, the effectiveness of DBT in a randomized control trial was in response to a multi-component intervention, making it unclear which components or combination of components were essential and which were not. For example, are all four of the types of skills taught in DBT (mindfulness, emotional regulation, interpersonal effectiveness, and distress tolerance) equally important? The lesson that may be drawn is that suicide prevention requires more complex, multi-dimensional approaches that impact the person's life in multiple spheres.

The strategies utilized in DBT can be divided into acceptance and change strategies. We are used to thinking of psychotherapeutic interventions as efforts at change, and Linehan (1993) has pointed out that much of behavior therapy is really a technology of change. Emphasis on acceptance strategies has been much more recent. In DBT, skills training modules in mindfulness and distress tolerance are considered acceptance strategies, while modules in emotional regulation and interpersonal effectiveness are considered change strategies. Distress tolerance strategies include skills focusing on simply surviving the crisis, not solving the underlying problems but, simply and profoundly, staying alive until the intensity of the wish to die diminishes. Another example of an acceptance skill is radical acceptance. Much in life cannot be changed, it can only be accepted. The death of a loved one and traumas that took place in the past are examples of events that can only be accepted, they cannot be changed.

While the precise balance between acceptance and change responsible for the effectiveness of DBT cannot be determined with certainty based on current evidence, it is worth noting that the importance of acceptance is a recurring theme in the literature on the psychotherapy of suicide risk. In her book, *Waking Up*, Terry Wise describes her psychotherapy before and after a near lethal suicide attempt. She describes the progression of "…making the unendurable, manageable…" (2003) In his book, *Autopsy of a Suicidal Mind*, the father of suicidology, Edwin Shneidman (2004) described how he would have approached working with a patient who had died by suicide, and whose mother had come to Shneidman trying to find some understanding of her tragic loss. In describing to her how he would have tried to work with her son if he had had the opportunity, Shneidman stated. "Together, he and I would redefine and fine-tune our understanding that, in actual practice, 'unbearable' and 'intolerable' really mean barely bearable and somehow tolerable... Hopefully, he could come to do what Emperor Hirohito ordered his overwhelmed people to do at the end of World War II: to suffer the insufferable and to endure the unendurable —and to live." (p. 163).

> **The importance of acceptance is a recurring theme in the literature on the psychotherapy of suicide risk**

DBT requires constantly balancing validation and problem solving. Validation, the empathetic valuing and support for the patient's own experience, is a core component for any therapeutic relationship, and is likely to be particularly important in working with those who are suicidal. However, validation, as critical as it is, needs to be balanced with helping patients solve the problems that are making them suicidal in the first place. Linehan emphasizes that prolonged focus on either validation or problem solving is unlikely to be effective (1993). The therapist must be attuned enough to the patient's needs and observant enough of the patient's response to therapeutic interventions to be able to know when each is necessary.

Regarding specific mechanisms of change, while cognitive behavior therapy or DBT may place greater emphasis on either changing cognition or regulating emotion as the driving engine for behavior change, these differing emphases are relatively subtle, as cognition, emotion, and behavior are all clearly in a dynamic interplay in each model of treatment.

The findings of the Fleischmann et al. (2008) study showing a reduction in deaths by suicide utilizing a combination of an ED intervention and post ED follow up, when considered in conjunction with the findings of Motto (1976) and Carter et al. (2005), suggest that sustained follow up contact may play a key role.

4.6   Efficacy and Prognosis

Several randomized controlled trials (RCTs) of DBT have demonstrated the treatment's effectiveness. The initial study found DBT to be more effective than treatment-as-usual (TAU) in treatment of suicidal patients who met diagnostic criteria for borderline personality disorder (Allmon et al., 1991). Those receiving DBT, compared to TAU, were significantly less likely to engage in suicide attempts or self harm, and when they did engage in suicidal behaviors, undertook less medically severe acts. Those receiving DBT were also less likely to be hospitalized, had fewer days in hospital, and had higher scores on global and social adjustment. In a second RCT focusing on treatment of women with borderline personality disorder and co-morbid substance abuse, Linehan et al. (1999), replicated the original study, and also found that DBT was more effective than TAU at reducing drug abuse. Koons et al. (2001) randomly assigned women veterans diagnosed with borderline personality disorder to either DBT or TAU. Unlike the original studies of Linehan et al. (1991, 1993), subjects were not required to have a recent history of suicidal behavior. Those receiving DBT showed significant reductions in suicidal ideation, depression, hopelessness, and anger compared to TAU. DBT has even shown in a RCT to be superior to an "expert treatment" control condition (Linehan et al., 2006). Efficacy with largely male populations of chronically suicidal patients requires further validation.

A recent RCT by Greg Brown and colleagues (2005) also demonstrated a reduction in suicide attempts by utilizing a 10-session cognitive therapy intervention with adults who had recently attempted suicide. Participants in the cognitive therapy group were 50% less likely to reattempt than those in the usual care group. Similarly, the RCT by Slee et al. (2008) found reductions in reoccurrence of suicidal behavior in a group of 15–35 year olds who had recently engaged in either a suicide attempt or an episode of self-harm without suicidal intent.

Since there is not yet evidence based on RCTs that these treatments, promising as they are in reducing suicide attempts, will also prevent deaths by suicide, it is prudent to plan with the patient for the potential recurrence of suicidality. Booster sessions are one reasonable way to do this, although not yet the subject of significant research. The significant evidence showing the effectiveness of non-demanding letters or postcards (Carter et al., 2005; Motto & Bostrum, 2001) suggests that this simple, low cost intervention be incorporated into clinical practice, and the results of the Fleischmann et al. study (2008) showing a reduction in deaths by suicide using an ED intervention plus follow up model strongly supports the incorporation of such follow up activities into all treatments for suicidal patients.

Clinicians must be prepared for the recurrence of suicidality

4.7   Variations and Combinations of Methods

4.7.1   Medication and Psychotherapy

Psychotherapy and pharmacotherapy are frequently used in combination when treating suicidal patients. One advantage of using both in combination is that this typically involves two different providers and it is wise to utilize a team approach when working with high-risk suicidal patients, so that ongoing consultation can occur.

As previously noted, there is research currently regarding the utility of at least three different types of medication. For two; lithium with bipolar patients and onanxapin with schizophrenia, there is some evidence of effectiveness, although the lithium research does not include a full scale, prospective RCT, and the research on onanxapin showed an impact on suicide behavior generally, rather than on deaths by suicide specifically.

For the third type of medication, there has been a firestorm of controversy regarding the use of SSRIs, particularly among youths. The controversy is regarding whether SSRIs might increase the risk of suicide among youths, or whether they decrease suicide risk. SSRIs are commonly used in the treatment of depression; indeed, they have been one of the most frequently prescribed medications in the U.S.

One complexity in any analysis of the relationship between SSRIs and suicidality is that SSRIs are used with many youths (and adults) who are at risk for suicide. It is therefore unclear if reports of suicidality following the onset of treatment result from the underlying disorder or are side effects of the medication.

The controversy over the possible role of SSRIs came to prominence first in England, where the British drug regulating agency ruled that paroxetine (Paxil) should not be used by English physicians for treatment of youths because of evidence of suicidality without evidence of effectiveness to outweigh potential risks. The ruling did not include fluoxetine (Prozac) because studies did exist showing effectiveness for treatment of depression among youths. Much of this work was based on reanalysis of the pharmaceutical industries' original data. There were no completed suicides in the data set, but some evidence of increased suicidal ideation or behavior. In the wake of the British decision, in the U.S., the FDA convened a series of hearings with much anecdotal testimony from people believing SSRIs caused suicides of a loved one. In the FDA analysis, for every 100 youth who received placebo, two became suicidal, but for those treated with SSRIs four out of every 100 became suicidal (FDA, 2006). Ultimately, the FDA issued a "black box warning" on the prescription of SSRIs to youths (excluding Prozac). The black box warning emphasized what should have been standard practice in treating persons at risk for suicide, careful monitoring. As a result, the prescription rates of SSRIs have decreased. Some have argued that the decrease in SSRI prescriptions has led to an increase in youth suicide (Gibbons et al., 2007).

It is important to remember that the black box warning does not recommend against the use of SSRIs, but instead calls for the careful monitoring for suicidality in the days and weeks following the start of antidepressant treatment, the kind of careful monitoring that should be routine when treating all patients at risk for suicide. The availability of medication as a potential treatment modality for those at risk for suicide should be routinely reviewed at the start of treatment as part of an informed consent for treatment, with referral available to a psychiatrist or other health professional skilled in psychopharmacology who can discuss with the patient in detail the potential benefits and risks.

4.7.2   Working With Families

The issue of the appropriate role of individual and family interventions is of particular importance in working with those at risk for suicide. Busch et al. (2003) have emphasized the importance of health professionals communicating and coordinating with family, as frequently patients hospitalized for suicide risk may not tell a clinician they are thinking about suicide, but may have said something to family members that warrants having concern. Similar findings by Barnes et al. (2001) with near lethal suicide attempters underscore the importance of working with families. The American Association of Suicidology has published the *AAS Recommendations for Inpatient and Residential Patients Known to be at Elevated Risk for Suicide*, which contains numerous recommendations relevant to working with families in inpatient and residential settings (see Table 13). These recommendations, however, are equally applicable to high-risk patients in outpatient settings. They strongly encourage the incorporation of families as meaningful members of the treatment team.

Table 13
Excerpted AAS Family-Focused Recommendations:

A) The availability of the family and other sources of support should be assessed, as well as their willingness and ability to provide such support.

B) A family session should routinely be recommended.

C) Both the patient and the family or significant others should be given instruction regarding suicide and its associated risk, including, but not limited to, the following: warning signs of suicide, the increased risk for suicide during hospital passes or following discharge; the need for medication and other treatment adherence; explanation of how psychiatric symptoms may impair judgment; explanation of the need for the patient to avoid use of intoxicants and how intoxicants increase risk; the need for the removal of the means for suicide, and the particular risk associated with firearms.

D) The patient and family or significant others should be given explicit instructions on how to access the treating physician or therapist regarding questions, observations, or concerns, and should be given information regarding how to access treating clinicians after office hours and any limitations on their availability. Emergency phone numbers that are available 24 hours a day, 7 days a week, such as psychiatric emergency services and crisis lines, should also be given.

E) If family members or significant others are asked to assist in the outpatient monitoring of risk, specific instructions should be given, including action steps to be taken in the event of felt concern or the development of a crisis. Consideration should be given to providing these in writing, as oral instructions may be difficult to recall accurately in the midst of a crisis.

F) Where permitted by law, and with the patient's written permission, the patient's family members or significant others should be alerted to the patient's history of suicidal thinking, feeling, behavior, and nonfatal suicide attempts.

Adapted from the *American Association of Suicidology Recommendations for Inpatient and Residential Patients Known to be at Elevated Risk for Suicide*. Available at www.suicidology.org

There are many reasons to involve the family and/or significant others routinely in the care of suicidal persons. Too often, clinicians involve families only when they see a specific indication. Rather than needing a specific indication, families should be involved in the treatment of suicidal persons routinely, and only not involved if there is a specific contraindication, such as abuse.

4.7.3   Treatment of Adolescents

As with treatments for many problems, treatments developed for adults cannot be assumed to be applicable to adolescents without adaptation. A version of DBT has been developed for adolescents, and preliminary results have been positive (Miller, Rathus, & Linehan, 2007). Using a quasi-experimental design, adolescent DBT was found to reduce suicidal ideation, reduce rates of psychiatric hospitalization, and increase treatment completion when compared to treatment as usual. The adolescent DBT model involves the family in skills training, and, like DBT for adults, includes both a group and an individual component. For a thorough review of current empirically based intervention with suicidal adolescents, see *Adolescent Suicide: Assessment and Intervention,* by Berman et al. (2006).

Family involvement is of particular importance in the treatment of adolescents at risk for suicide. Communication about the level of suicide risk to parents is extremely important along with the plan for addressing that risk and instructions for how to respond to escalations in suicidality. In some states there are legal requirements for such disclosures. As pointed out by Berman et al. (2006), suicidal adolescents in treatment rarely self-refer. Most often, they are brought to treatment by parents or guardians. Therefore, engaging families and keeping them involved and informed is essential for successful treatment to take place. Even if individual psychotherapy is the major intervention utilized, family intervention will need to take place as well.

There is evidence that a group at particularly high risk for suicidal behavior, particularly suicide attempts, is adolescents who are gay, lesbian bisexual, or transgendered (D'Augelli et al., 2005). A particular high risk time may be the period when a youth discloses his/her sexual orientation to his/her family. Family support and connectness appears to be particulary important in protection against suicide attempts (Eisenberg & Resnick, 2006).

4.7.4   Individual and Group Treatment

For many years clinical lore advised against the use of group modalities with those who had attempted suicide or were otherwise at risk for suicide. Fear of patients inadvertently harming each other through sharing the details of their suicide attempts was likely a part of this fear. However, the success of DBT in combining individual and group treatment has convincingly demonstrated that the addition of group modalities can be potentially of great value. In DBT, the group focus is on skills training and the fears regarding contagion or negative influences are dealt with by providing the skills training with clear guidelines on maintaining the focus on the teaching of skills, with suicidal communications dealt with by rapid referral to the individual therapist upon the ending of the group.

Also noteworthy is an increasing focus in recent years on peer support services. Peer support groups and other peer support services exist for those struggling with mental illness. Those that focus on suicide attempt survivors and others at risk for suicide exist but are not yet widely available, nor have they as yet been rigorously evaluated. However, given the demonstrated difficulties in engaging those at risk for suicide in formal mental services, peer support services hold promise.

4.8   Problems in Carrying Out the Treatments

4.8.1   Problems in Communication and Information Gathering

In a unique project sponsored by the American Foundation for Suicide Prevention, a registry of 36 patients who died by suicide while in treatment was created utilizing questionnaires and case narratives submitted by therapists who had lost a patient to suicide and were willing to share information about the treatment (Hendin, Haas, Maltsberger, Koestner, & Szanto, 2006). While the findings from this study may not be representative of all patients who died by suicide while in treatment, the results are nonetheless instructive. One pattern was the lack of active communication among all treatment providers involved in the care of the patients. Although 23 patients had been in treatment with another provider previously, communication between the current and previous therapist was described as rare. (Hendin et al., 2006). In four instances, there was lack of communication between a therapist and a psychiatrist who were treating the patient together. Such lack of communication prevents the sharing of potentially critical information. While it is unclear if the frequency of consultation with past treatment providers and the obtaining of prior records among this sample is any worse than in common clinical practice, it is clear that obtaining such information is particularly important when treating high-risk patients. Similarly, consultation with other providers is widely regarded as part of the standard of care for treating suicidal patients (Bongar, 2002). Consultation provides support and an additional perspective for therapists facing some of the most difficult clinical decisions they are called upon to make. It is for this reason that Linehan (1993) has built a consultation team into DBT as an essential component of the treatment.

An additional problem in treatment highlighted in the registry was the lack of treatment for substance abuse. In 11 of the 36 cases, obvious substance abuse was never treated (Hendin et al., 2006).

In many cases of suicide, obvious substance abuse was never treated

4.8.2   Problems in Continuity of Care

For all clinicians, losing a patient to suicide is one of the greatest traumas they will encounter in their professional lives. Yet, until recently, very little information was available in the U.S. regarding how often suicide occurred among those receiving mental health treatment. In Great Britain, the National Confidential Inquiry into Suicide and Homicide by People with Mental Illness (Appleby et al., 2001) found that approximately one quarter of all people who died by suicide in England, Wales, Scotland, and Northern Ireland had been in contact with mental health services in the year before death. Suicide on inpatient units accounted for 10–16%, depending on the country. An even larger number, 23–30% died within three months of discharge from an inpatient unit, with a peak in the first two weeks following discharge. Just under one third of suicides in the community missed their final outpatient sessions. An assertive effort was made to re-establish contact in about half of these cases. This type of data, so critical for mental health service delivery, has not previously been available in the U.S., on a national level or on a scale as large as a state. Yet this information is critical for guiding suicide prevention efforts, such as enhancing risk assessment capacities, improving continuity of care, and preventing drop out from treatment. However, no large scale data from the U.S. were available until the recent publication of data from the National Violent Death Reporting System (NVDRS).

Looking at data across 13 states, Karch et al. (2006) found rates of current mental health treatment ranged from 32.8% for white non-Hispanics, to 15.2% for Hispanics. Results from Sanford et al. (2006) indicated that 58% of females in North Carolina but only 32.5% of males were receiving current mental health treatment. Similar data were also found in the state of Maryland. Women aged 45–59 years had the highest rate of suicide among all age groups for females, and 74% of them were in mental health treatment at the time of their suicide. In contrast, 33% of men in that same age group who died by suicide were in mental health treatment. Powell et al. (2006) interpret these results as meaning that improving mental health care for women is an indicated suicide prevention strategy, but may be less so for men. In contrast, for men, promoting help seeking might be more important.

Data of particular importance are available from the State of South Carolina, where NVDRS data have been linked to a human resources data base to allow precise information to be available regarding the most recent health care contact prior to death by suicide. Of 491 suicides that took place in the state during the year 2004, 20 suicides occurred within 7 days of discharge from an emergency department or inpatient unit, and 27 more died within 30 days of discharge (Weis, Bradberry, Carter, Ferguson, & Kozareva, 2006). This means that in the state of South Carolina, more than 4% of all suicides took place within 7 days of discharge from an acute care setting, and almost 10% of all suicides took place within 30 days of discharge from such a setting. Like the findings from Great Britain, these findings underscore the importance of further research into discharge decision making, risk assessment protocols, and continuity of care following discharge to help us reduce this tragic toll.

Almost 10% of all suicides took place within 30 days of discharge from an acute care setting

Acute treatments are generally regarded as essential when working with suicidal patients, but such treatments are typically short term, and while they may lessen suicide risk at times of exceptionally high risk, they are unlikely to eliminate suicide risk entirely. This makes the follow-up to acute care particularly important. The Institute of Medicine found that those at risk for suicide are "insufficiently followed after acute treatment" (Goldsmith et al., 2002). Given this well documented increased risk after inpatient discharge and other acute care discharge, careful follow-up is clearly indicated. Outpatient therapists, who may be used to having weekly psychotherapy sessions with their patients, or outpatient clinics, which may have long waiting lists and demands for therapist's time, should schedule appointments for discharged patients as soon as possible after discharge, within 48 hours if possible, but always within a week.

4.8.3   Problems in Initial Risk Assessment

Additional information from South Carolina indicated that 18.5% of suicides were receiving outpatient mental health services in the public sector (Weiss et al., 2006). No information was available about those who might have been seen in private practice settings. Nine were seen within a week of their suicide, two within 24 hours. Of those being seen in the outpatient public mental heath system, the median number of visits was 8, meaning that many of these persons were relatively new to the mental health system. This suggests that many suicides that took place by patients within mental health systems may occur with patients who have not yet established a meaningful therapeutic relationship with a clinician. It may also be that either the initial assessment of suicide risk was incomplete, or the relationship was not deep enough for the patient to reveal the depth of their despair or the content of their ideation. This would underline the importance of a thorough, comprehensive suicide risk assessment taking place within the context of a developing, collaborative relationship. The South Carolina data also pointed to the existence of a subgroup of suicide deaths by patients with very large numbers of contacts, possibly pointing to a clustering of multiple suicide attempters.

> **Many suicides may occur with patients who have not yet established a meaningful therapeutic relationship with a clinician**

4.8.4   Problems in Collaboration

A critical issue in the treatment of persons at risk for suicide is whether the patient is able to be a collaborative partner in keeping himself or herself alive. The combination of high, acute risk and the inability to establish a collaborative relationship is an indication for hospitalization. Breakdowns in collaboration must be addressed as a very high priority. There are times when a clinician will need to act unilaterally to safeguard the patient, making emergency decisions either without the patient's consent, or even against the patient's explicit wishes. Intervening with an intoxicated, suicidal patient with access to lethal means would be a clear example. However, this should always be a last resort. It is imperative that clinicians working with suicidal patients not practice "defensive" mental health. As Simon emphasizes, "Good clinical care is always the best risk management" (Simon, 2004). In addition, we have distressingly little empirical data to assist us in determining what the impact of involuntary or coercive interventions are on long term suicide risk. Interventions that decrease suicide risk in the coming days or weeks (e.g., involuntary hospitalization) may inadvertently increase suicide risk in the future in those cases in which our patients are reluctant to share with us their suicidal thoughts and urges for fear of involuntary intervention. When this occurs, we are less able to assist them in their struggle to stay alive. This may be particularly true for patients whose competence to make decisions is not obviously compromised by intoxication or active psychosis.

Linehan builds into her treatment model a mechanism for continuing to work on collaboration between patient and therapist throughout the treatment. She introduces the concept of "therapy interfering behavior" (Linehan, 1993), which is anything that patients might do that would make the therapist want to terminate therapy and anything that the therapist might do that would make the patient want to drop out. Therapy interfering behavior is second only to suicidal behavior in the DBT hierarchy of targets in treatment (Linehan, 1993).

Drop out and poor follow-up are also issues that need to be addressed. At risk patients who fail to show up for appointments should be actively outreached. For patients at risk who drop out of treatment, it is recommended that therapists incorporate as a standard part of their treatment protocol for high-risk patients the episodic mailing of non-demanding follow-up letters as per the findings of Motto and Bostrum (2001) and Carter et al. (2005). The potential significance of routinely incorporating such a simple intervention, both within systems of care and in private practices, is highlighted by the findings by Gibbs et al. (2004), who describe the poor attendance rate of the suicide attempt population, where only 30–60% attend follow-up appointments.

Therapists should send patients who drop out of treatment non-demanding follow-up letters

4.9   Multicultural Issues

There are important cultural differences in suicide rates, frequency of suicide attempts, and attitudes toward suicide (see Table 14). Despite this, little systematic research attention has been paid to the clinical implications of these differences in suicidal behavior and attitudes toward suicide among the major ethnic and cultural groups in the U.S. (Range et al., 1999). This lack of focus is unfortunate as sociocultural norms can either facilitate or inhibit suicidal behavior (Orbach, 1997). Important questions remain to be answered. For example, why do African American women have one of the lowest suicide rates in the nation? What promotes this level of resilience, what protective factors are present that

---

Table 14
Multicultural disparities in suicidal behavior in the U.S.

According to the Centers for Disease Control (2008d), there are marked disparities present regarding suicidal behavior among ethnic and cultural groups. These include:

- Among American Indians/Alaska Natives ages 15- to 34-years, suicide is the second leading cause of death.

- Suicide rates among American Indian/Alaskan Native adolescents and young adults ages 15 to 34 (21.4 per 100,000) are 1.9 times higher than the national average for that age group (11.5 per 100,000).

- Hispanic female high school students in grades 9–12 reported a higher percentage of suicide attempts (14.9%) than their White, non-Hispanic (9.3%) or Black, non-Hispanic (9.8%) counterparts.

lead to such low rates despite significant socioeconomic stress and historical trauma? Conversely, what leads rates of suicide to be so high among American Indian youth, and why is there such marked tribal variability?

An analysis of the risk of suicide among Hispanic females aged 12 to 17 years conducted during the 2000 National Household Survey on Drug Abuse found they were at heightened risk of suicidal behavior compared to other youths (SAMHSA, 2003). Youths were asked during the interview whether they had thought seriously about killing themselves or tried to kill themselves during the 12 months before the survey interview. In addition, Hispanic females were less likely to have received treatment for their suicidal thoughts or attempts, with only 32% having received treatment. And, for those girls who did receive treatment they were less likely than other youths to have had their suicidality be the reason for treatment, making it less likely that even those who received treatment received specific evidence-based treatments focused on their suicide risk.

A byproduct of the early developmental stage of research into suicide and suicide prevention is that, despite the clear prominence of cultural issues in suicide, there is little specific information available about effective treatments for culturally diverse groups.

The lack of research data is particularly prominent among the cultural group with the highest rate of youth suicide in the U.S.: American Indians and Alaska Natives. There is little information available about the efficacy of either DBT or cognitive behavior therapy with either group. The most encouraging results have come from the Western Athabaskan Natural Helpers Program, which demonstrated a 61% decrease in suicide attempts among youth during 12 years of implementation (May et al., 2005). This program worked with Natural Helpers, members of the tribal community who provided lay counseling to those identified as being at risk, with therapy by professionals reserved for those assessed at more serious risk.

Rotherman-Borus, Piacentini, Cantwell, Belin, & Song (2000) studied an ED intervention with Latina females. Young female suicide attempters and their families were interviewed in the emergency room, shown a psychoeducational videotape, and encouraged to enroll in outpatient psychotherapy. Those who received the intervention were more likely to follow-up in treatment. The intervention also incorporated training of emergency department staff.

Nadine Kaslow and colleagues have studied risk for suicidal behavior among low income African American women, and found that risk factors include physical and non-physical partner abuse, childhood maltreatment, posttraumatic stress, hopelessness, psychological distress, and drug abuse(2002). These findings underline the importance, both in outpatient and emergency settings, of screening for both suicide risk and domestic violence, whenever one of them is present.

A relationship between domestic violence and suicidality among low income African American women has been found

5

Case Vignette

Julie

This is a brief case study of a 28-year-old Greek-American woman with several suicide attempts. She entered outpatient treatment at a community mental health center following a psychiatric hospitalization for one of these attempts. Because of her history of prior suicide attempts as well as frequent suicidal ideation, she was referred for admission to the dialectical behavior therapy (DBT) treatment program. Her inpatient clinician had obtained the client's permission to both contact this clinician and forward her inpatient records. During the consultation with her inpatient clinician, her suicidal history, precipitants for self-destructive actions, suicide risk factors, and diagnostic and treatment history were reviewed.

At the initial session, with the therapist's encouragement, Julie described the pain that she has been experiencing that led to her suicidal behavior. The therapist encouraged her to tell her story, weaving into their conversations questions designed to help him understand how she had come to the brink of self-destruction, and to obtain the information necessary for a comprehensive risk assessment. Julie was experiencing significant psychosocial stress, including being unable to continue to work at a professional position at which she had previously excelled. She also was estranged from most members of her family. She experienced intense negative emotions in response to these stressors, including most prominently anxiety, guilt, and shame. In addition to these major stressors, she also responded with great emotional intensity to the stresses and strains of daily life. These emotions would frequently propel self-destructive behavior, including episodes of self-cutting. These episodes were frequently accompanied by suicidal ideation.

Julie was oriented to DBT. Like many patients she responded positively to being told that her emotional sensitivity was not under her cognitive control, and was something she needed to learn to accept and cope with, rather than suppress and castigate herself for. She was relieved to learn that her sensitivity was not her fault, but worried that she had to learn to better tolerate and regulate her emotions without resort to suicidal behavior. She agreed to accept as a goal of treatment that she would work to keep herself alive, no matter what, during the one-year treatment commitment to DBT. She agreed to attend both weekly individual therapy and a weekly DBT skills training group. She worked with the therapist on a safety plan, which included calling the therapist prior to engaging in suicidal behavior and calling the psychiatric emergency service if the therapist was not available. When it emerged during the interview that the patient carried razor blades in her purse "in case I need them," she agreed to give them to the therapist. Julie would not allow her family to be contacted, but did agree to have a close friend, who lived nearby, be called.

At the beginning of treatment Julie was cutting herself several times per week. She struggled to remain in the DBT skills training group for the entire session. She would be able to remain in the group when skills were being taught, but when it was her turn to report on how she had used the skills in the past week, she would experience a flood of panic and flee from the group. Then, ashamed of how she reacted and fearful of how her therapist would respond, she would experience suicidal ideation and cut herself.

There were also episodes in which her cutting was not limited to a single cut, but where she would make multiple cuts, or would have multiple episodes of cutting within a period of hours. The therapist closely consulted with Julie's psychiatrist and on two occasions where her cutting escalated (one of which culminated in an overdose), she was hospitalized.

Following each episode of self-harm, Julie and the therapist would conduct a behavioral chain analysis, a detailed examination of the flow of events, thoughts, emotions and behaviors leading to the episode. The functional relationship among these would be explored. For example, her cutting and overdosing functioned as escape behavior. They distracted Julie from her surging dysphoric emotions, reducing the pain. The self-destructive behavior was being negatively reinforced by the momentary pain reduction. Even her suicidal ideation functioned as a distractor from her intense emotions. In fact, suicidal thoughts appeared to be an automatic response to negative emotions. On her diary cards, which she filled out daily, suicidal ideation was found to be present every day, although the frequency and intensity varied from day to day. Because of the daily experience of suicidal thoughts, suicidal ideation alone was not considered an indication for hospitalization. Single episodes of cutting, even when accompanied by suicidal ideation, were also not considered indications for hospitalization.

Hospitalization was an aversive experience for Julie, who experienced a deep sense of failure with each hospital admission. Psychiatric admissions also tended to reinforce her view of herself as crazy and incompetent, and decreased her sense of self-efficacy in being able to cope with her own emotions. Psychiatric hospitalizations were thus used sparingly with Julie, and only when necessary to interrupt an escalating series of self-destructive behaviors.

Treatment focused on helping Julie learn how to cope with intense negative emotions without resorting to self destructive behavior. Expressions of suicidality were found to be triggered by intolerable thoughts and emotions. Identifying these emotions and encouraging Julie to sit for a moment with these feelings utilizing mindfulness skills was a major focus of therapy during individual sessions. Julie and her therapist were able to identify that strong emotions, particularly sadness and shame, triggered panic and anxiety, which in turn triggered a tremendous urge to escape. By helping Julie to focus her attention on the feelings that she usually fled from, Julie gradually learned that these feelings could be tolerated. This constituted a form of exposure therapy. The therapist was able to provide immediate support to Julie as she sat with these feelings.

Outside of sessions an emphasis was placed on the distress tolerance skills taught in the skills training group. These "crisis survival strategies" included distraction techniques, including holding an ice cube and focusing all of her attention on the cold sensations. Further analysis of her reaction to many interpersonal situations, including being in the DBT Skills Training Group, revealed that when she was flooded with panic she would feel that she couldn't breathe unless she escaped the situation. Cognitive behavior techniques for the treatment of anxiety disorders, such as diaphragmatic breathing, were incorporated into the treatment to help her manage her anxiety.

While Julie continued to experience suicidal thoughts on a daily basis, the frequency of cutting, overdosing, and psychiatric hospitalizations gradually decreased. When episodes of cutting did occur they tended to be associated with efforts to return to work. Julie made several such attempts.. These efforts invariably increased the amount of anxiety and panic she experienced and the likelihood of suicidal behavior if she did not succeed in coping with the job demands. On several occasions she had to leave work due to the anxiety, leading to an escalating suicidal crisis. The behavioral principle of shaping was used to help Julie look for work that did not have intensive social or interpersonal demands, to heighten the likelihood that she could keep the job, and lessen the likelihood of self-destructive behavior.

The telephone was used extensively to help coach Julie through crisis periods without resorting to self-destructive behavior. Typically, if Julie could reach her therapist, he could walk her through the skills she had been taught, and cutting or overdosing could be averted. If the therapist could not be reached, Julie had, as part of her safety plan, the phone number for the mental health center's psychiatric emergency service. Julie's response to psychiatric emergency service intervention in the first few months of treatment was quite varied as she was extremely sensitive to being a "burden" to the system and would tend to react to even subtle cues that she was taking too much time or that the emergency clinician had other people to respond to, by apologizing, getting off the phone, and cutting herself.

In order to help Julie deal with the emergency service more effectively, the therapist assisted Julie in writing out instructions for the emergency service regarding what she would find most useful in getting her through a crisis. This plan was then placed in the emergency service's "at risk" file which was reviewed by emergency clinicians at the start of each shift.

By the end of one year of DBT Julie was able to regularly attend skills group and while the frequency of self-destructive episodes and psychiatric hospitalization were clearly decreased, persistent suicidal ideation and occasional episodes of self-harm remained. Julie, her therapist and her psychiatrist decided she would remain in DBT until self-destructive behavior could be eliminated. Ultimately, for Julie, the goal is not simply the absence of self-destructive behavior, but rather achieving a life that she feels is worth living.

6

Case Example

Intake Evaluation and Treatment Plan

Identifying Data:
Dana is a 17-year-old, Caucasian female who was referred by her mother who accompanied her to the intake evaluation. This is her first application for outpatient treatment.

Chief Complaint:
Her boyfriend's suicide.

History of Present Problem:
Two weeks ago, the patient's boyfriend died by suicide. She had been unaware of any prior suicidal thinking on his part. At the time that he killed himself, she had just been on the telephone with him.

They had had a disagreement earlier, but had just resolved it. She had asked to speak to a mutual friend who was at the boyfriend's house at the time. While the patient and the friend were on the telephone, there was a noise and the friend told the patient that the boyfriend had shot himself, and told her to get help. She did not believe him at first. When the friend put the phone next to her boyfriend she heard a low moaning sound. She then hung up in a panic and called the police who went to the house. She did not hear anything for a few hours and then was informed that her boyfriend was dead. The patient has internalized blame for this tragedy and feels that he killed himself because of her. This is because she had been told by the friend that her boyfriend had made a statement shortly before the phone call, referring to her and saying "I love her too much. I can't take it." She also felt guilty that she did not believe that he had shot himself, and did not immediately call for help. However, she remains extremely confused as she is unable to recall anything from the telephone conversation itself that would seem to even hint at suicide. For this reason she wonders whether it could have been an accident, or even whether the friend may have shot him. (There are apparently rumors to this effect circulating at the local high school.)

In the days following the death, Dana was mostly at home alone with her sister. Her parents were at a retreat. They were in telephone contact with Dana and asked her if she needed them to come home but she told them "no." However, she later acknowledged to them, and to this clinician, that she was having suicidal ideation. Dana felt that her boyfriend wanted her to join him. She had thought about carbon monoxide poisoning and about cutting her wrists, and finally developed a plan where she would take an overdose of Prozac, which had been prescribed for her by her family physician to help her through the bereavement. The day she picked for the suicide attempt was one week prior to this appointment and one day before her parents returned from their retreat. She states that she had the bottle of pills in front of her and wrote a suicide note. But then she began to think about what her parents would go through if she killed herself. She also thought that at least now she had memories of her boyfriend and if she killed herself she didn't know whether she would still have those memories. Finally, she was also afraid that if she took the overdose she might end up as a vegetable. She ultimately aborted the attempt by deciding that if her boyfriend really wanted her to join him, then he would find a way to tell her. She didn't really feel that he would be likely to somehow materialize and so in an important sense this was a way of deciding not to die by suicide. However, she does experience him as being close by and she talks to him frequently. After her parents arrived home, she told them that she had thought of suicide, and they made arrangements for this appointment. Since that time she has continued to have suicidal thoughts, though she reports these thoughts are weaker and less frequent than previously, and are easier to distract herself from. She reports that she has not had any thoughts about suicide today. When asked if talking about her boyfriend's death in the therapy session made her think about suicide, she said "no."

Past Psychiatric History:
Dana has no past episodes of psychiatric illness. There also does not appear to be any past history of drug or alcohol abuse. There is no family history of depression or suicide, although there was an uncle who had some kind of emotional disturbance, the nature of which is unknown at present.

Mental Status:
Dana was oriented to person, place, and time. She exhibited no unusual motor behaviors. Her long- and short-term memory seemed intact. Intelligence was judged to be at least average. Judgment and insight seemed good. Mood appeared to be depressed as would be expected in someone recently bereaved. She admitted to occasional suicidal ideation, but no homicidal ideation. Thought processes were logical and coherent. There was no evidence of any thought disorder or delusional thinking. She denied auditory or visual hallucinations.

Assessment:
Axis I   – V62.82 Bereavement
          – 309.00 Adjustment Disorder with Depressed Mood
Axis II   – None
Axis III – None
Axis IV   – Severity of psychosocial stressors, severe to extreme, 5 to 6 death of boyfriend by suicide
Axis V   – GAF – current, 53
            Highest in past year, 80

Dana presents with depressed mood and suicidal ideation which clearly had its onset at the time of her boyfriend's suicide. What would probably best capture the essence of Dana's clinical condition at this time is to consider this a bereavement that is complicated because of the presence of suicidal ideation. The death of a loved one through suicide often results in a complicated bereavement with a wide range of intense emotional responses and in this instance her reaction is intensified by the fact that she had been on the telephone with him at the time he died by suicide.

In evaluating Dana's level of suicidal risk, several factors are important. She has no past history of suicide attempts or of suicidal ideation. There is no family history of suicide. She is not drug or alcohol involved. She did have both suicidal intent and a suicide plan approximately one week ago. The presence of suicide intent was indicated by her writing a suicide note and she made preparations for a suicide attempt by placing the medication in front of her that she was going to use in an overdose. The potential lethality of the aborted attempt was mild to moderate. A factor lessening the extent of suicidal risk is that at the moment when her suicidal intent was the greatest, during the initial overwhelming feelings of shock and distress, Dana was able to cognitively work through and evaluate the advantages of living over dying, and was able to choose life. Another positive sign is that since that time, while there has remained some episodic suicidal ideation, it has been lessening and has been without intent or clear plan. Additionally, it appears clear that Dana's suicidal ideation is intricately linked with her coming to terms with the reality of the loss of her boyfriend. She wants to kill herself only so she could join him, and if this reunion fantasy were not possible she states she would not want to kill herself. This suggests that through therapy she would come more to terms with the reality of this loss, and would then give less consideration to her self-described "fantasy" of joining him. It is significant that at this point in time she states that she would only kill herself if her boyfriend literally appeared to her and told her to kill herself so she could join him. Since the patient is not at all psychotic and she is well aware that this would not happen, and since she specifically denies that she would act on such ideation if he, for example, appeared to her in a dream, the overall level of suicidal risk at this moment appears low.

Treatment Plan:

Goal 1: Suicidal Ideation: The goal will be the elimination of all suicidal ideation within a two-month time frame. The means for attaining this goal were discussed with the patient and with her mother. Hospitalization was included in the review of treatment alternatives as the safest option. Since her present level of suicidal risk did not seem high, both Dana and her mother felt that she did not need hospitalization and would prefer instead an outpatient treatment option. Outpatient psychotherapy seems to be a feasible alternative considering the overall low level of suicidal risk currently, and that the patient and mother understand the benefits and risk of outpatient therapy compared to hospitalization. Given that Dana was still experiencing some episodic suicidal ideation, another appointment was made for later in the week. Weekly sessions were to follow afterwards. Dana and her mother were given the telephone number for the psychiatric emergency service and Dana was able to clearly state that she would call before acting on any suicidal ideation. Dana's mother agreed that she would lock up all medication in the house. Both Dana and her mother reported that there were no firearms in the house. Consultation was obtained with the staff psychiatrist who concurred with the plan.

Goal 2: Complicated bereavement: While it is hoped that Dana will be completely free of suicidal ideation within two months with weekly psychotherapy sessions, it is unlikely that this would be sufficient to help her work through completely the complexity of her bereavement. Indicators of improvement will be when she ceases to blame herself for her boyfriend's suicide, when the ruminative preoccupation with his death decreases substantially (i.e., decrease of 75% of such statements), and when she is able to invest her energies again in age appropriate social and dating activities. The time frame for achieving these goals would be four months, with weekly psychotherapy sessions.

7

Further Reading

American Psychiatric Association. (2003). *Practice guideline for the assessment and treatment of patients with suicidal behavior*. Arlington, VA: Author.

The only currently existing set of professional guidelines for assessing and treating suicidal patients.

Berman, A., Jobes, D., & Silverman, M. (2006) *Adolescent suicide: Assessment and intervention.* Washington, DC: American Psychological Association.

Widely regarded as the most authoritative text on the assessment, management and treatment of adolescents at risk for suicide. A comprehensive and empirically based review.

Bongar, B. (2002). *The suicidal patient: Clinical and legal standards of care*. Washington, DC: American Psychological Association.

The definitive source on standards of care in treating suicidal patients.

Jobes, D. (2006). *Managing suicidal risk: A collaborative approach*. New York: Guilford Press.

Treatment manual for the Collaborative Assessment and Management of Suicidality Project. Useful for a wide range of mental health professionals regardless of theoretical orientation.

Joiner, T. (2005). *Why people die by suicide,* Cambridge, MA: Harvard University Press.

A masterful integration of the research on why people die by suicide, leading to a potentially groundbreaking conceptualization of the central roles of suicidal desire and suicidal capacity.

Linehan, M. M. (1993). *Cognitive behavioral treatment of borderline personality disorder*. New York: Guilford Press.

Comprehensive treatment manual for dialectical behavior therapy. The most thorough, science-based resource currently available for treating chronically suicidal patients with borderline personality disorder.

Rudd, M. D., Joiner, T., & Rahab, M. H. (2001). *Treating suicidal behavior: An effective time limited approach*. New York: Guilford Press.

Empirically supported treatment manual for time-limited psychotherapeutic treatment of suicidal behavior.

Shea, S. (2002). *The practical art of suicide assessment: A guide for mental health professionals and substance abuse counselors*. Hoboken, NJ: John Wiley.

A major contribution to the art and science of suicide risk assessment.

Shneidman, E. S. (1996). *The suicidal mind*. New York: Oxford University Press.

A concise introduction to the contributions of the founder of the first suicide prevention programs in the United States.

8

References

Allmon, D., Armstrong, H. E., Heard, H. L., Linehan, M. M., & Suarez, A. (1991). Cognitive-behavioral treatment of chronically parasuicidal borderline patients. *Archives of General Psychiatry, 48*, 1060–1064.

American Association of Suicidology. (2005). United States suicide statistics 2005. Retrieved online from www.suicidology.org

American Association of Suicidology. (2008). *AAS recommendations for inpatient and residential patients known to be at elevated risk for suicide.* Retrieved online from www.suicidology.org

American Psychiatric Association. (2000). *Diagnostic and statistical manual of mental disorders (4th ed., text revision).* Arlington, VA: American Psychiatric Association.

American Psychiatric Association. (2003). *Practice guideline for the assessment and treatment of patients with suicidal behavior.* Arlington, Virginia: American Psychiatric Association.

Appleby, L., Shaw, J., Amos, T., McDonnell, R., Harris, C., McCann, K., et al. (1999). Suicide within 12 months of contact with mental health services: National clinical survey. *British Medical Journal, 318*, 1235–1239.

Appleby, L., Shaw, J., Amos, T., McDonnell, R., Harris, C., & McCann, K. (2001). *Safety first: five- year report of the national confidential inquiry into suicide and homicide by people with mental illness.* London: Department of Health Publications.

Asberg, M. (1997). Neurotransmitters and suicidal behavior: The evidence from cerebrospinal fluid studies. *Annals of the New York Academy of Sciences, 836*, 158–181.

Aseltine, R. H., & DeMartino, R. (2004). An outcome evaluation of the SOS suicide prevention program. *American Journal of Public Health, 94*, 446–451.

Baraff, L. J., Janowicz, N., & Asarnow, J. R. (2006). Survey of California emergency departments about practices for management of suicidal patients and resources available for their care. *Annals of Emergency Medicine, 48*(4), 452–458.

Barnes, L., Ikeda, R., & Kresnow, M. (2001). Help seeking behavior prior to nearly lethal suicide attempts. *Suicide and Life Threatening Behavior, 32*, 68–75.

Beautrais, A. L. (2004). Further suicidal behavior among medically serious suicide attempters. *Suicide and Life threatening Behavior, 34*, 1–11.

Beautrais, A. L. (2007). The contribution to suicide prevention of restricting access to methods and sites. *Crisis, 28*(Suppl. 1), pp. 1–3.

Beck, A. T. (1996). Beyond belief: A theory of modes, personality, and psychopathology. In P. Salkovskis (Ed.), *Frontiers of cognitive therapy* (pp. 1–25). New York: Guilford.

Beck, A. T., Brown, G., & Steer, R. (1989) Prediction of eventual suicide in psychiatric inpatients by clinical rating of hopelessness. *Journal of Consulting and Clinical Psychology, 57*, 309–310.

Beck, A. T., Davis, J. H., Frederick, C. J., Perlin, S., Pokorny, A., Schulman, R. E., et al. (1973). In H. Resnick & B. Hawthorne (Eds.), *Suicide prevention in the 70s.* Washington, DC: US Government Printing Office.

Beck, A. T., Kovacs, M., & Weissman, A. (1979). Assessment of suicidal ideation: The scale for suicidal ideation. *Journal of Consulting and Clinical Psychology, 47*, 343–352.

Beck, A. T., Steer, R. A., Kovacs, M., & Garrison, B. (1985). Hopelessness and eventual suicide: A 10 year prospective study of patients hospitalized with suicidal ideation. *American Journal of Psychiatry, 142,* 559–563.

Bennett, B., Bricklin, P., Harris, E., Knapp, S., VandeCreek, L., & Younggren, J. (2006). *Assessing and managing risk in psychological practice: An individualized approach.* Rockville, MD: The Trust.

Berman, A., Jobes, D., & Silverman, M. (2006). *Adolescent suicide: Assessment and intervention* (2nd ed.). Washington, DC: American Psychological Association.

Bolton, I. (with Mitchell, C.) (1984). *My son, my son: A guide to healing after death, loss or suicide.* Atlanta, GA: Bolton Press.

Bongar, B. (2002). *The suicidal patient: Clinical and legal standards of care.* Washington, DC: American Psychological Association.

Bongar, B., Maris, R., Berman, A., & Litman, R. (1998). Outpatient standards of care and the suicidal patient. In B. Bongar, A. Berman, R. Maris, M. Silverman, E. Harris, & W. Packman (Eds.), *Risk management and suicidal patients* (pp. 4–33). New York: Guilford.

Borges, G., Angst, J., Nock, M., Ruscio, A. M., Walters, E., & Kessler, R. (2006). A risk index for 12-month suicide attempts in the National Comorbidity Survey Replication (NCS-R). *Psychological Medicine, 36,* 1747–1757.

Bostwick, J. M., & Pancratz,V. S. (2000). Affective disorders and suicide risk: A Reexamination. *American Journal of Psychiatry, 157,* 1925–1932.

Brent, D. (2001). Firearms and suicide. *Annals of the New York Academy of Sciences, 932,* 225–240.

Brent, D., Baugher, M., Birmaher, B., Kolko, D., & Bridge, J. (2000). Compliance with recommendations to remove firearms in families participating in a clinical trial for adolescent depression. *Journal of the American Academy of Children and Adolescent Psychiatry, 39,* 1226–1228.

Brent, D., Perper, J., Moritz, G., Allman, C., Friend, A., Roth, C., et al. (1993a). Psychiatric risk factors for adolescent suicide: A case control study. *Journal of the American Academy of Child and Adolescent Psychiatry, 33,* 1080–1086.

Brent, D., Perper, J., Moritz, G., Baugher, M., Roth, C., Balach, L., et al. (1993b). Stressful life events, psychopathology and adolescent suicide: A case control study. *Suicide and Life Threatening Behavior, 23,* 179–187.

Brown, G., Jeglic, E., Henriques, G., & Beck, A. (2006). Cognitive therapy, cognition, and suicidal behavior. In T. Ellis (Ed.), *Cognition and suicide: Theory, research and therapy* (pp.53–74). Washington, DC: American Psychological Association.

Brown, G., Ten Have, T., Henriques, G., Nie, S., Hollander, J., & Beck, A. (2005). Cognitive therapy for the prevention of suicide attempts. *Journal of the American Medical Association, 294,* 563–570.

Bruce, M. L., Ten Have, T. R., Reynolds, C. F. III, Katz, I., Schulberg, H. C., Mulsant, B. H., et al. (2004). Reducing suicidal ideation and depressive symptoms in depressed older primary care patients: A randomized controlled trial. *Journal of the American Medical Association, 291*(9), 1081–1091.

Busch, K. A., Fawcett, J., & Jacobs, D. G. (2003). Clinical correlates of inpatient suicide. *Journal of Clinical Psychiatry, 64*(1), 14–19.

Carter, G., Clover, K., Whyte, I., Dawson, A., & D'Este, C. (2005). Postcards from the edge: Randomized controlled trial of an intervention using postcards to reduce repetitions of hospital treated deliberate self poisoning. *British Medical Journal, 10,* 1–5.

Centers for Disease Control. (2007). Suicide trends among youth and young adults aged 10-24 years-United States, 1990–2004. *Morbidity and Mortality Weekly Report, 56,* 906–908.

Centers for Disease Control. (2008a). Deaths: Final data for 2005. *National Vital Statistics Reports, 56*(10), 1–121.

Centers for Disease Control. (2008b). Surveillance for violent deaths – national violent death reporting system, 16 states, 2005. *Morbidity and Mortality Weekly Report, 57*(SS 03), 1–43, 45.

Centers for Disease Control. (2008c). Youth risk behavior surveillance – United States 2007. *Morbidity and Mortality Weekly Review, 57*(SS 04), 1–131.

Cheng, A. T. A. (1995). Mental illness and suicide. *British Journal of Psychiatry, 170*, 441–446.

Cherpitel, C., Borges, G., & Wilcox, H. (2004). Acute alcohol use and suicidal behavior: a review of the literature. *Alcoholism: Clinical and Experimental Research, 28*, 18–28.

Chessick, C. A., Perlick, D. A., Miklowitz, D. J., Kaczynski, R., Allen, M. H., Morris, C. D., & Marangel, L. B. (2007). Current suicidal ideation and past suicide attempts of bipolar patients as influences on caregiver burden. *Suicide and Life Threatening Behavior, 37*, 482–491.

Cipriani, A., Pretty, H., Hawton, K., & Geddes, J. (2005). Lithium in the prevention of suicidal behavior and all-cause mortality in patients with mood disorders: A systematic review of randomized trials. *American Journal of Psychiatry, 162*, 1805–1819.

Connor, K. R., Beautrais, A. L., & Conwell, Y. (2003). Risk factors for suicide and medically serious suicide attempts among alcoholics: Analyses of Canterbury suicide project data. *Journal of the Study of Alcoholism, 64*, 551–554.

Connor, K. R., & Duberstein, P. R. (2004). Predisposing and precipitating factors for suicide among alcoholics: empirical review and conceptual integration. *Alcoholism: Clinical and Experimental Research, 28*, 6–17.

Connor, K. R., Duberstein, P. R., & Conwell, Y. (1999). Age-related patterns of factors associated with completed suicide in men with alcohol dependence. *American Journal of Addictions, 8*, 312–318.

Cooper, J., Kapur, N., Webb, R., Lawlor, M., Guthrue, E., Mackway-Jones, K., & Appleby, L. (2005). Suicide after deliberate self-harm: A 4-year cohort study. *American Journal of Psychiatry, 162*, 297–303.

D'Augelli, A. R., Grossman, A. H., Salter, N. P., Starks, M. T., Vasey, J. J., & Sinclair, K. O. (2005). Predicting the suicide attempts of lesbian, gay, and bisexual youth. *Suicide and Life-Threatening Behavior, 35*, 646–660.

The Dougy Center. (2001). *After a suicide: A workbook for grieving kids.* Portland, OR: The Dougy.

Dube, S. R., Anda, R. F., Felitti, V. J., Chapman, D. P., Williamson, D. F., & Giles, W. H. (2001). Childhood abuse, household dysfunction, and the risk of attempted suicide throughout the life span: Findings from the Adverse Childhood Experiences Study. *Journal of the American Medical Association, 286*(24), 3126–3127.

Dunne, E. (1992). Following a suicide: Postvention. In B. Bongar (Ed.), *Suicide: Guidelines for assessment, management and treatment* (pp. 221–234). New York: Oxford University Press.

Dyches, B., Johnsen, G., & Oh, M. (2002). The impact of mobile crisis services on the use of community-based mental health services. *Research on Social Work Practice, 12*(6), 751–763.

Eisenberg, M.E., & Resnick, M.D. (2006). Suicidality among gay, lesbian and bisexual youth: The role of protective factors. *Journal or Adolescent Health 39*(5), 662–668.

Ellis, T., & Newman, C. F. (1996). *Choosing to live: How to defeat suicide through cognitive therapy.* Oakland, California: New Harbinger.

Farrow, T., Simpson, A., & Warren, H. (2002). The effects of the use of "no-suicide contracts" in community crisis situations: The experience of clinicians and consumers. *Brief Treatment and Crisis Intervention, 3,* 241–246.

Fergusson, D. M., Woodward, L. J., & Horwood, L. J. (2000). Risk factors and life processes associated with the onset of suicidal behavior during adolescence and early adulthood. *Psychological Medicine, 30*(1), 23–29.

Fine, C. (1999). *No time to say goodbye.* Mansfield, OH: Main Street Books.

Fleischmann, A., Betolote, J.M., Wasserman, D., DeLeo, D., Bolhari, J., Botega, N.J. et al. (2008). Effectiveness of brief intervention and contact for suicide attempters: A randomized controlled trial in 5 countries. *Bulletin of the World Health Organization, 86,* 703–709.

Geller, J. L., Fisher, W. H., & McDermeit, M. (1995). A national survey of mobile crisis services and their evaluation. *Psychiatric Services, 46,* 893–897.

Gibb, S., Beautrais, A., & Ferguson, D. (2005). Mortality and further suicidal behavior after an index suicide attempt: A 10 year study. *Australia and New Zealand Journal of Psychiatry, 39,* 95–100.

Gibbons, R. D., Brown, C. H., Hur, K., Marcus, S. M., Bhaumik, D. K., Erkens, J. A., et al. (2007). Early evidence on the effects of regulators' suicidality warnings on SSRI prescriptions and suicide in children and adolescents. *American Journal of Psychiatry, 164*(9), 1356–1363.

Gibbons, R. D., Brown, C. H., Hur, K., Marcus, S. M., Bhaumik, D. K., & Mann, J. J. (2007). Relationship between antidepressants and suicide attempts: An analysis of the veterans health administration data sets. *American Journal of Psychiatry, 164*(7), 1044–1049.

Giffin, R., Erickson, S., McHugh, M., Wheatley, B., Dharshi, A., Madhani, S., & Trenum, C. (2006). *The future of emergency care.* Washington, DC: National Academies Press.

Goldney, R. D. (1998). Variations in suicide rates: The tipping point. *Crisis, 19,* 136–138.

Goldsmith, S., Pellmar, T., Kleinman, A., & Bunney, W. (2002). *Reducing suicide: A national imperative.* Washington, DC: National Academies Press.

Gould, M. S., Kalafat, J., Harris Munfakh, J. L., & Kleinman, M. (2007). An evaluation of hotline outcomes, part 2: Suicide callers. *Suicide and Life-Threatening Behavior, 37*(3), 338–352.

Griffith, G. (2005). *Will's choice.* New York: Harper Collins.

Gutheil, T. G. (1990). Argument for the defendant-expert opinion: death in hindsight. In R.I. Simon (Ed.), *Review of clinical psychiatry and the law* (pp. 335–339). Washington, DC: American Psychiatric Association.

Hawton, K. (2005). *Prevention and treatment of suicidal behavior.* New York: Oxford University Press.

Hendin, H., Haas, A., Maltsberger, J., Koestner, B., & Szanto, K. (2006). Problems in psychotherapy of suicidal patients. *American Journal of Psychiatry, 163,* 67–72.

Ho, T. P. (2003). The suicide risk of discharged psychiatric patients. *Journal of Clinical Psychiatry, 64* (6), 702–707.

Hugo, M., Smout, M., & Bannister, J. (2002). A comparison in hospitalization rates between a community-based mobile emergency service and a hospital-based emergency service. *Australian and New Zealand Journal of Psychiatry, 36,* 504–508.

Inskip, H., Harris, E., & Barraclough, B. (1998). Lifetime risk of suicide for affective disorder, alcoholism, and schizophrenia. *British Journal of Psychiatry, 172,* 35–37.

Jamison, K. R. (1999). *Night falls fast.* New York: Random House.

Jobes, D. (2006). *Managing suicidal risk: A collaborative approach.* New York: Guilford.

Jobes, D., Eyman, J., & Yufit, R. (1995). How clinicians assess suicide risk in adolescents and adults. *Crisis Intervention and Time Limited Treatment, 2,* 1–12.

Joiner, T. (2005). *Why people die by suicide.* Cambridge, MA: Harvard University Press.

Joiner, T., Kalafat, J., Draper, J., Stokes, H., Knudson, K., Berman, A., et al. (2007). Establishing standards for the assessment of suicide risk among callers to the national suicide prevention lifeline. *Suicide and Life Threatening Behavior, 37*(3), 353–365.

Joint Commission on the Accreditation of Health Care Organizations (2007). *National patient safety goals.* Chicago, IL: Joint Commission on the Accreditation of Health Care Organizations.

Joint Commission on the Accreditation of Health Care Organizations (2008). *Sentinel event statistics - June 30, 2008.* Chicago, IL: Joint Commission on the Accreditation of Health Care Organizations.

Karch, D. L., Barker, L., & Strine, T. W. (2006). Race/ethnicity, substance abuse and mental illness among suicide victims in 13 states: 2004 data from the National Violent Death Reporting System. *Injury Prevention, 12*(Suppl. II), 22–27.

Kaslow, N. J., Thompson, M. P., Okun, A., Price, A., Young, S., Bender, M., et al. (2002). Risk factors for suicide attempts among African-American women. *Journal of Consulting and Clinical Psychology, 70*, 311–319.

Kleespies, P. M., Penk, W. E., & Forsyth, J. P. (1993). The stress of patient suicidal behavior during clinical training: Incidence, impact and recovery. *Professional Psychology: Research and Practice, 24*, 293–303.

Knox, K. L., Litts, D. A., Talcott, G. W., Feig, J. C., & Caine, E. D. (2003). Risk of suicide and related adverse outcomes after exposure to a suicide prevention program in the U.S. Air Force: Cohort study. *British Medical Journal, 327*, 1376–1381.

Koons, C. R., Robins, C. J., Tweed, J. L., Lynch, T. R., Gonzalez, A. M., Morse, J. Q., et al. (2001). Efficacy of dialectical behavior therapy in women veterans with borderline personality disorder. *Behavior Therapy, 32*, 371–390.

Kruesi, M. J. P., Grossman, J., Pennington, J. M., Woodward, P. J., Duda, D., & Hirsch, J. G. (1999). Suicide and violence prevention: Parent education in emergency department. *Journal of the American Academy of Child and Adolescent Psychiatry, 38*(3), 250–255.

Lewis, L. M. (2007). No suicide contracts: A review of what we know. *Suicide and Life-Threatening Behavior, 37*, 50–57.

Lezine, D. (with Brent, D.) (2008). *Eight stories up: An adolescent chooses hope over suicide.* New York: Oxford University Press.

Linehan, M. M. (1981). *Suicidal Behaviors Questionnaire.* Unpublished manuscript: University of Washington, Seattle.

Linehan, M. M. (1993). *Cognitive behavioral treatment of borderline personality disorder.* New York: Guilford Press.

Linehan, M. M. (2008). Suicide intervention research: A field in desperate need of development. *Suicide and Life Threatening Behavior, 38*, 483–485.

Linehan, M. M., Comtois, K., Murray, A., Brown, M., Gallup, R., Heard., H., et al. (2006). Two year randomized control trial and follow up of dialectical behavior therapy vs. therapy by experts for suicidal behaviors and borderline personality disorder. *Archives of General Psychiatry, 63*, 757–766.

Linehan, M. M., Goodstein, J., Nielsen, S., & Chiles, J. (1983). Reasons for staying alive when you are thinking of killing yourself: The Reasons for living inventory. *Journal of Consulting and Clinical Psychology, 51*, 276–286.

Linehan, M. M., Schmidt, H., Dimeff, L. A., Kanter, J. W., Craft, J. C., Comtois, K. A., et al. (1999). Dialectical behavior therapy for patients with borderline personality disorder and drug-dependence. *American Journal on Addiction, 8*, 279–292.

Linn-Gust, M. (2001). *Do they have bad days in heaven?* Atlanta, GA: Bolton Press.

Luoma, J. B., Martin, C. E., & Pearson, J. L. (2002). Contact with mental health and primary care providers before suicide: A review of the evidence. *American Journal of Psychiatry, 159*, 909–916.

Maris, R. W. (1981). *Pathways to suicide: A survey of self-destructive behavior*. New York: Oxford University Press.

Maris, R. W. (1992). The relationship of nonfatal suicide attempts to completed suicides. In R.W. Maris, A. Berman, J. Maltsberger, & R. Yufit (Eds.), *Assessment and prediction of suicide*. New York: Guilford Press.

Maris, R. W. (2007). A comment on Robert D. Goldney's "A historical note on suicide during the course of treatment for depression." *Suicide and Life Threatening Behavior, 37,* 600–601.

May, P., Serna, P., Hurt, L., & DeBruyn, L. (2005). Outcome evaluation of a public health approach to suicide prevention in an American Indian tribal nation: 1988–2002. *American Journal of Public Health, 95,* 1238–1244.

McCaig, L. F., & Nawar, E. N. (2006). *National hospital ambulatory medical care survey: 2004 emergency department summary. Report no. 372, Advance data from vital and health statistics*. Hyattsville, MD: National Center for Health Statistics.

McNiel, D. E., Gregory, A. L., Lam, J. N., Binder, R. L., & Sullivan, G. R. (2003). Utility of decision support tools for assessing acute risk of violence. *Journal of Consulting and Clinical Psychology, 71,* 945–953.

Meltzer, H. Y. (1999). Suicide and schizophrenia: Clozapine and the InterSePT study. International Clozaril/Leponex Suicide Prevention Trial. *Journal of Clinical Psychiatry, 60*(Suppl. 12), 47–50.

Meyers, M., & Fine, C. (2006). *Touched by suicide: Hope and healing after suicide*. New York: Gotham Books.

Miller, A. L., Rathus, J. H., & Linehan, M. M. (2007). *Dialectical behavior therapy with suicidal adolescents*. New York: Guilford.

Miller, M. C. (1999). Suicide prevention contracts: Advantages, disadvantages, and an alternative approach. In D. G. Jacobs (Ed.), *The Harvard medical school guide to suicide assessment and intervention* (pp. 463–481). San Francisco: Jossey-Bass.

Molnar, B. E., Buka, S. I., & Kessler, R. C. (2001). Child sexual abuse and subsequent psychopathology: results from the National Comorbidity Study. *American Journal of Public Health, 91*(5), 753–760.

Moscicki, E. K. (2001). Epidemiology of completed and attempted suicide: Toward a framework for prevention. *Clinical Neuroscience Research, 1,* 310-323.

Moskos, M. A., Olson, L. M., Halbern, S., Keller, T., & Gray, D. (2005). Utah youth suicide study: Psychological autopsy study. *Suicide and Life Threatening Behavior, 35*(5), 536–546.

Motto, J. (1976). Suicide prevention for high risk patients who refuse treatment. *Suicide and Life Threatening Behavior, 6*(4), 223–230.

Motto, J., & Bostrum, A. (2001). A randomized control trial of post crisis suicide prevention. *Psychiatric Services, 52,* 828–833.

Murphy, G. E., & Robbins, E. (1967). Social factors in suicide. *Journal of the American Medical Association, 199,* 81–86.

Murphy, G. E., Armstrong, J. W., Hermele, S. I., Fischer, J. R., & Clendenin, W. W. (1979). Suicide and alcoholism : Interpersonal loss confirmed as a predictor. *Archives of General Psychiatry, 36,* 65–69.

Nock, M., Borgas, G., Bromet, E., Alonso, J., Angermeyer, M., Beautrais, A., et al. (2008). Cross national prevalence and risk factors for suicidal ideation, plans and attempts. *British Journal of Psychiatry, 192,* 98–105.

Office of the Ombudsman for Mental Health and Mental Retardation, State of Minnesota (2002). *Suicide prevention alert,* Final Recommendations: November 15, 2005.

Orbach, I. (1997). A taxonomy of factors related to suicidal behavior. *Clinical Psychology: Science and Practice, 4,* 208–224.

Owens, D., Horrocks, J., & House, A. (2002). Fatal and non-fatal repetition of self-harm: Systematic review. The British Journal of Psychiatry, *181*, 193–199.

Pirkola, S. P., Isometsa, E. T., Heikkenin, M. E., Henriksson, M. M., Marttunen, M. J., & Lonnqvist, J. K. (1999). Female psychoactive substance dependent suicide victims differ from males – results from a nationwide psychological autopsy study. *Comprehensive Psychiatry, 40*, 101–107.

Posner, K., Oquendo, M., Gould, M., Stanley, B., & Davies, M. (2007). Columbia classification algorithm of suicide assessment (C-CASA): Classification of suicidal events in the FDA's pediatric suicidal risk analysis of anti-depressants. *American Journal of Psychiatry, 164*, 1035–1043.

Pottick, K., McAlpine, D., & Andelman, R. (2000). Changing patterns of psychiatric inpatient care for children and adolescents in general hospitals, 1988–1995. *American Journal of Psychiatry, 157*, 1267–1273.

Powell, V., Barber, C., Hedegaard, H., Hempstead, K., Hull-Jilly, D., Shen, X., et al. (2006). Using NVDRS data for suicide prevention: promising practices in seven states. *Injury Prevention, 12*(Suppl. II), 28–32.

Preuss, U. W., Schuckit, M. A., Smith, T. L., Danko, G. P., Buckman, K., Bierut, L., et al. (2002). Comparison of 3190 alcohol-dependent individuals with and without suicide attempts, *Alcoholism: Clinical & Experimental Research, 26*(4), 471–477.

Range, L. M., & Knott, E. C. (1997). Twenty suicide assessment instruments: Evaluation and recommendations. *Death Studies, 21*, 25–58.

Range, L. M., Leach, M., McIntyre, D., Posey-Deters, P., Marion, M., Kovac, S., et al. (1999). Multicultural perspectives on suicide. *Aggression and Violent Behavior, 4*, 413–430.

Rogers, J., & Oney, K. (2005). Clinical use of suicide assessment scales: Enhancing reliability and validity through the therapeutic relationship. In R. Yufit & D. Lester (Eds.), *Assessment, treatment and prevention of suicidal behavior* (pp. 7–27). Hoboken, NJ: John Wiley and Sons.

Rotheram-Borus, M. J., Piacentini, J., Cantwell, C., Belin, T. R., & Song, J. (2000). The 18-month impact of an emergency room intervention for adolescent female suicide attempters. *Journal of Consulting and Clinical Psychology, 68*(6), 1081–1093.

Roy, A., Rylander, G., & Sarchiapone, M. (1997). Genetics of suicide: family studies and molecular genetics. *Annals of the New York Academy of Sciences, 836*, 135–157.

Rudd, M. D., Joiner, T., & Rahab, M. H. (2001). *Treating suicidal behavior: An effective time limited approach.* New York: Guilford Press.

Safer, D. J., & Zito, J. M. (2007). Do antidepressants reduce suicide rates? *Journal of the Royal Institute of Public Health, 121*, 274–277.

Sanford, C., Marshall, S. W., Martin, S. I., Coyne-Beasley, T., Walker, A. E., Cook, P. J. et al. (2006). Deaths from violence in North Carolina: How deaths differ in females and males. *Injury Prevention, 12*(Supp. II), 10–16.

Schuckit, M. A., Tipp, J. E., Bergman, M., Reich, W., Hesselbrock, V. M., & Smith, T. L. (1997). Comparison of induced and independent major depressive disorders in 2,945 alcoholics. *American Journal of Psychiatry, 154*, 948–957.

Scott, R. L. (2000). Evaluation of a mobile crisis program: Effectiveness, efficiency and consumer satisfaction. *Psychiatric Services, 51*, 1153–56.

Shea, S. (2002). *The practical art of suicide assessment: A guide for mental health professionals and substance abuse counselors.* Hoboken, NJ: John Wiley and Sons.

Shneidman, E. S. (1996). *The suicidal mind.* New York: Oxford University Press.

Shneidman, E. S. (2004). *Autopsy of a suicidal mind.* New York: Oxford University Press.

Shulsinger, R., Kety, S., Rosenthal, D., & Wender, P. (1979). A family study of suicide. In M.

Schou & E. Stromgren (eds.), *Origins, prevention and treatment of affective disorders* (pp. 277–287). New York: Academic Press.

Silverman, M. M., Berman, A. L., Sanddal, N. D., O'Carroll, P. W., & Joiner, T. E. (2007a). Rebuilding the Tower of Babel: A revised nomenclature for the study of suicide and suicide related behaviors Part 1: Background, rationale, and methodology. *Suicide and Life-Threatening Behavior, 37*, 248–263.

Silverman, M. M., Berman, A. L., Sanddal, N. D., O'Carroll, P. W., & Joiner, T. E. (2007b). Rebuilding the Tower of Babel: A revised nomenclature for the study of suicide and suicide related behaviors Part 2: Suicide-related ideations, communications, and behaviors. *Suicide and Life-Threatening Behavior, 37*, 264–277.

Simon, R. (2004). *Assessing and managing suicide risk: Guidelines for clinically based risk management.* Washington, DC: American Psychiatric Association.

Simon, R. (2006). Imminent suicide: The illusion of short-term prediction. *Suicide and Life Threatening Behavior, 36,* 296–301.

Simon, R. (2007). Gun safety management with patients at risk for suicide. *Suicide and Life Threatening Behavior, 37,* 518–525.

Simon, T., Swann, A., Powell, K., Potter, L., Kresnow, M., & O'Carroll, P. (2001). Characteristics of impulsive suicide attempts and attempters. *Suicide and Life Threatening Behavior, 32,* 49–59.

Skog, O. (1991). Alcohol and suicide: Durkheim revisited. *Acta Sociologica, 34,* 193–206.

Slee, N., Garnefski, N., van der Leeden, R., Arensman, E., & Spinhoven, P. (2008). Cognitive-behavioral intervention for self-harm. *British Journal of Psychiatry, 192,* 202–211.

Stanley, B., & Brown, G. (2008). *Safety planning: A brief intervention to mitigate suicide risk.* Manuscript submitted for publication.

Stanley, M., & Stanley, B. (1989). Biochemical studies in suicide victims: Current findings and future implications. *Suicide and Life Threatening Behavior, 19,* 30–42.

Styron, W. (1990). *Darkness visible.* New York: Vintage Books.

Substance Abuse and Mental Health Services Administration. (2003). *National Survey on Drug Use and Health: Risk of Suicide among Hispanic Females Aged 12-17.* Retrieved from www.oas.samhs.gov

Substance Abuse and Mental Health Services Administration. (2006). Suicidal Thoughts, Suicide Attempts, Major Depressive Episode, and Substance Abuse Among Adults. *The OAS Report, 34.* Retrieved from www.oas.samhs.gov/2k6/suicide/suicide.htm

Substance Abuse and Mental Health Services Administration. (2006). National Survey on Drug Use and Health: Suicidal Thoughts among Youths Aged 12 to 17 with Major Depressive Episode. *The NSDUH Report, September 9.* Retrieved from www.oas.samhs.gov/2k5/suicide/suicide.htm

Teasdale, J. D., Segal, Z. V., Williams, J. M. G., Ridgeway, V., Soulsby, J., & Lau, M. (2000). Prevention of relapse/recurrence in major depression by mindfulness-based cognitive therapy. *Journal of Consulting and Clinical Psychology, 68,* 615–623.

U.S. Department of Health and Human Services, Food and Drug Administration, www.fda.gov.

U.S. Department of Health and Human Services. (2001). *National Strategy for Suicide Prevention: Goals and Objectives for Action.* Rockville, MD, DHHS Publication No. SMA-3517.

U.S. Department of Health and Human Services. (2003). *The President's New Freedom Commission Report, Achieving the Promise: Transforming Mental Health Care in America.* DHHS Publication No. SMA-03-3832.

Van der Sande, R., van Rooijen, E., Buskens, E., Allart, E., Hawton, K., van der Graaf, Y., et al. (1997). Intensive in-patient and community intervention versus routine care after attempted suicide: a randomised controlled intervention. *British Journal of Psychiatry*, *171*, 35–41.

Vajani, M., Annest, J., Crosby, A., Alexander, J., Millet, L. (2007). Nonfatal and fatal self-harm injuries among children aged 10–14 years: United States and Oregon, 2001–2003. *Suicide and Life Threatening Behavior, 37*(5), 493–506.

Walsh, B. W. (2006). *Treating self-injury*. New York: Guilford.

Waterhouse, J., & Platt, S. (1990). General hospital admission in the management of parasuicide: A randomised controlled trial. *British Journal of Psychiatry*, *156*, 236–42.

Weis, M. A., Bradberry, C., Carter, L. P., Ferguson, J., & Kozareva, D. (2006). An exploration of human services system contacts prior to suicide in South Carolina: An expansion of the South Carolina National Violent Death Reporting System, *Injury Prevention, 12*(Suppl. II), 17–21.

Welu, T. C. (1977). A follow-up program for suicide attempters: Evaluation of effectiveness. *Suicide and Life Threatening Behavior, 7,* 17–30.

Williams, J. M., Barnhofer, T., Crane, C., & Dugan, D. (2006). The role of overgeneral memory in suicidality. In T. Ellis (Ed.), *Cognition and suicide: Theory, research and practice* (pp.173–192). Washington, DC: American Psychological Association.

Wise, T. (2004). *Waking up*. Oxnard, California: Pathfinder Publications.

World Federation for Mental Health (2006). *Building awareness-reducing risk: Mental illness and suicide*. Monograph of the WFMH International Experts Forum on Mental Illness and Suicide, March 30–31, 2006, Dulles, VA. Retrieved from www.wfmh.org/PDF/SuicideBody20%copy.pdf

World Health Organization, www.who.int/mental_health/prevention/suicideprevent/en/index.html

9

Appendices: Tools and Resources

The following tools and resources are found in the appendices:

Appendix 1: Outline for Suicide Consultation
Appendix 2: Decision Tree for Intervening with Suicidal Callers

Appendix 1: Outline for Suicide Consultation

I) **Reason for Referral:**

II) **History of Suicidal Thoughts, Feelings, and Behaviors**

1) *Precipitant for most recent episode of suicidality:*
   a) Family or other interpersonal precipitants
   b) Psychological/emotional precipitants
   c) Health precipitants
   d) Other precipitants, i.e., social, financial, etc.

2) *Psychological state during most recent episode of suicidality:*
   a) Mental Status Variables:
      Degree of disorientation versus ability to accurately test reality, (including psychosis, intoxication, etc.), insight, judgment, mood, affect, degree of perturbation, presence of psychiatric symptoms.
   b) Suicide Risk Variables
      Suicidal ideation including: frequency, intensity, intrusiveness, sense of felt control over ideation, degree of suicidal intent, thinking about methods, availability of method, degree of suicidal planning, preparatory behaviors, degree to which plans had been initiated into action, suicidal threats and communications, whether attempt made and rating of lethality, behaviors intended to aid rescue versus behaviors intended to conceal discovery.

3) *Protective factors:*
   Degree to which suicidal ideas or impulses have been able to be resisted, ability to tolerate distress, deal with ambivalence, tolerate frustration, future orientation, attitude toward help seeking, interpersonal connectedness, ability to sustain connectedness and hope in face of loss, impulse control, strength of therapeutic alliance.

4) *Vulnerabilities:*
   Loss of sustaining resource, psychiatric illness, modeling of suicide within the family and degree of identification, cognitive vulnerabilities, impulsivity.

5) *Past Suicide History*
   (List for each past suicidal attempt or episode of acute suicidality)
   a) Precipitants: family/interpersonal, cognitive, emotional/psychological, biological, social/financial.
   b) Suicidal state and behaviors: intent, degree of planning, rating of lethality, rescue-ability, degree of impulsivity, degree of perturbation, reaction to attempt.

6) *Consequences of Suicidal Behavior:*
   Functional analysis, interpersonal effects, relief vs regret.

III) Risk Assessment:

Summary of factors contributing to elevated risk: family/interpersonal, cognitive, emotional/psychological, biological, social, financial, psychiatric illness, suicide history.

Projected Risk for Suicide:
1) Imminent
2) Short-term
3) Long-term

Recommended intervention strategies to decrease suicidal risk: (include whenever possible treatment or intervention strategies specifically targeted to decreasing previously identified suicide risk factors). Interventions should be considered to alter both precipitants and vulnerabilities.

Appendix 2: Decision Tree for Intervening with Suicidal Callers

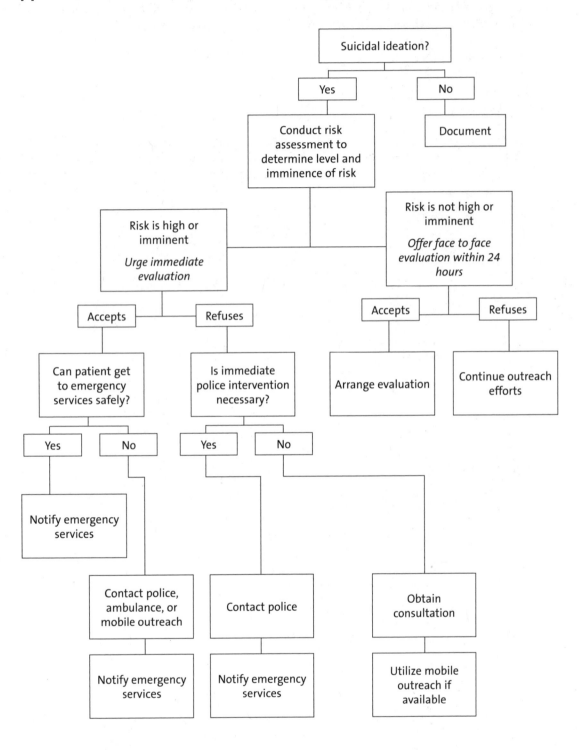

From: R.T. McKeon: *Suicidal behavior*